イディオム・アタック

# Idiom Attack

### ❸ Taking Action

Peter, Matthew & Jay 作

## About the Authors

### Peter N. Liptak  ピーター・N.リプタク

Peter N. Liptak came to Asia in 1995 to teach English, then started learning Korean and working as a writer and copywriter. As a poet and teacher of English, his desire to help people around the globe in their struggles with the untamed beauty of the English language has led to teaching at universities and the writing of language acquisition books. After finishing a Master's in Korean Studies at Yonsei University, Peter involved himself with several other writing projects including a series of children's books, a translation of Korean poetry into English and a website helping foreign nationals to become acclimated to Korea and its culture. Currently, Peter enjoys exploring the world while training for triathlons, mountain biking, and competing in ultra-marathons while raising money for orphans to experience outdoor activities.

ピーターN.リプタクは英語教師として1995年に韓国へ渡り、その後は韓国語の勉強をし、執筆者、コピーライターとして仕事を始めました。英語の不規則さから生まれる美しさを理解しようと苦戦する世界の人々の力になりたいと言う気持ちから、詩人でもある英語教師のピーターは大学で教え、語学習得の本を書くようになりました。ヨンセイ大学院での韓国研究の修士号を終えた今は、児童文学のシリーズ、韓国の詩の英訳と韓国文化を外国人に紹介するウェブサイトの作成に取り込んでいます。今、ピーターはトライアスロンとマウンテンバイクの練習をし、孤児のアウトドア活動を提供する慈善団体の資金集めのためにウルトラマラソンに参加しながら、世界中を飛び回っています。

### Matthew Douma  マシュー・ドーマ

Matthew Douma grew up in a small rural town in Southern Canada. Ever since his early childhood years, Matthew has had a deep interest in Asia and made his first visit when he was just fifteen years old. As an avid outdoorsman and adventurer, Matthew enjoys sports of all sorts including Taekwondo. Matthew also has a passion for mountain climbing, sailing and writing as hobbies. Residing in Seoul with his lovely wife Sun Hee and daughter Ennik, he works as an English education consultant and author of English educational material.

マシュー・ドーマは南カナダの小さな田舎町で育ちました。幼い頃から韓国へ強い関心を持ち、わずか15歳の時に初めて韓国を訪れました。アウトドア派の冒険好きなマシューはテコンドーを始め数多くのスポーツに参加しています。それと同時に、趣味としての登山と帆走そして著述業に熱中しています。美しい妻のサン・ヒーと娘のエニックとソウルで暮らし、英語教育コンサルタントと英語教材の著者として活躍しています。

### Jay Douma  ジェイ・ドーマ

An elementary school teacher since 1999, Jay enjoys writing stories and collaborating with his brother on creative projects. Currently teaching grade five and physical education in Ontario, Canada, Jay enjoys spending time with his wife Christa and daughter Emma at their home on Lake Erie when not working.

1999年から小学校の教師を勤めているジェイは執筆を得意とし、兄と一緒に創作活動に取り組んでいます。カナダのオンタリオで5年生の教師と体育の教師を勤めながら、エリー湖のそばの家で妻のクリスタと娘のエマと休暇を過ごします。

### A bow to our translator  翻訳者に一礼

Caroline Yuko Omura Eddis comes from a bilingual family and was educated in both Japan and the UK. After completing High School in Japan, she graduated from Durham University in England with a degree in English literature, French and Philosophy in 2008. She is now based in Japan working as a translator and interpreter of English, Japanese and French.

大村祐子キャロライン・エディスはバイリンガル家庭に育ち、英国と日本の両国で教育を受けました。日本の高校を卒業後、英文学、仏語、哲学を専攻した英国ダラム大学文学部を2008年に卒業、現在は日本で英和仏の翻訳・通訳者として活躍しています。

Special thanks to our Japanese editors and proofreaders:
Kenyu Makio and Kozue Kaise of K&K Co. in Victoria, Australia
Akiko O Eddis MA MITI in Osaka, Japan

日本人編集者、校正者へスペシャルサンクス
K&K. Co. より　牧尾健祐　＆　貝瀬梢　オーストラリア　ヴィクトリア州
エディス晶子　MA　MITI　日本　大阪

# Idiom Attack

### ❸ Taking Action

Peter, Matthew & Jay 作

# Getting Used to Idioms

英語慣用語に慣れよう

### Conquering idioms – A three-step training process

Idioms decorate the daily conversations of native English speakers in various ways. An idiom is a phrase in which two or more words come together to create a unique meaning that is different from the meaning of each of the individual words. Because the combination of words will seem peculiar to non-native speakers, it is quite difficult for foreigners to learn idioms. If your goal is to conquer English, you must conquer idioms (before they attack you).

This book includes about 300 frequently used idioms divided into 25 thematic chapters. The themes are key topics of English conversation used in daily life and business, for describing actions and expressing emotions. Each chapter introduces 10-15 idioms. The meaning of each idiom is explained in both English and Japanese. Example sentences help your understanding and use of the idioms. And to enable in-depth learning, this book includes a story that uses the idioms introduced in each chapter.

### Step 1. Learn the meaning of idioms through Japanese
Infer the meaning of the idioms inserted into Japanese sentences, and then take a look at how the idioms are used in example English sentences. This is an easier and more effective way to learn their meaning and use. In addition, the idioms are used in the Japanese sentence to help you recall them.

### Step 2. Confirm the use of idioms with the fill-in-the-blank section
Confirm the meaning of the idioms once again by filling in the blanks in additional example sentences. A translation right below each sentence and one or two words in the idiom presented as a clue enable you to easily complete the sentences and completely familiarize yourself with the idioms.

### Step 3. Practice the use of the idioms by reading a story
Each of the short, but interesting stories enables you to understand how idioms are used in real-life settings. You can increase your skill with idioms and even start to sound like a native speaker by practicing the story and answering the questions.

## 慣用語を征服しよう!－3段階の勉強法

英語を母国語として話す人は慣用語をさまざまな方法で使うことで、日常会話を飾り、表現豊かにします。イディオム（慣用語）とは2つ以上の単語を組み合わせることで、元の単語と異なる、新しい意味を生み出す用語です。英語のネイティブでない人にとっては、この見慣れない組み合わせは、覚えにくいものです。英語を征服したいなら、まずは慣用語をマスターして下さい（慣用語にアタックをされる前に…）。

この本では、よく使われる、英語の慣用語300語を、テーマ別に25章に分けて紹介しています。テーマは、日常生活と職場、または行動を起こす時や感情を表現する時に使う英会話の基本的な項目です。各章では10から15の慣用語を紹介しています。全ての慣用語の意味を英語と日本語の両方で説明しています。例文を参考にすると、慣用語の意味や使い方についてさらに分かりやすくなります。より深い理解や応用を目的として、慣用語が実際に使われている場面を各章の最後に紹介しています。

### ステップ1．日本語を通じて、慣用語の意味を理解する。
日本語の文章に入っている英語の慣用語の意味をまず推測して下さい。そして、英語の例文でどのように使われているかを見て下さい。これは意味や使い方を理解できる簡単で効果的な方法です。さらに、日本語の文章中に英語の慣用語が使われていることでその意味が思い出しやすくなります。

### ステップ2．穴埋め問題を解いて、慣用語の使い方を身に付ける。
新しい例文の穴埋めをすることで、慣用語の意味を再確認します。例文の下に記している訳と、慣用語の一部が既にヒントとして示されていることで、簡単に慣用語全体が思い出せ、慣用語が身近なものになります。

### ステップ3．ストーリーを読んで慣用語を使う練習をしよう。
おもしろい内容を短くまとめたストーリーを読むことで、慣用語が実際にどのように使われているかがはっきり分かります。ストーリーを読み込み、質問に答えることで、慣用語の実力をつけて、ネイティブのような響きを持たせて英語が話せるようになります。

# Preface

> 序文

*Idiom Attack – Taking Action* is a collection of nearly 300 North American idioms in usage today, arranged in a format that is both easy to read and understand, while creating a situational learning format with logical and independently dynamic subject and chapter themes that take the user directly to the subject they want to learn. Arranged in a series of 25 chapters, this text was designed as a learning resource for intermediate to advanced students of English, yet its language was deliberately kept simple enough to also be accessible to high beginners.

An idiom (or phrasal expression) is a set phrase of two or more words that when put together mean something different than the literal meaning of the individual words. As idioms are the idiosyncrasies of a language, they tend to be the most challenging for foreign learners to understand and for teachers to convey. Though complex, they can be indicative of some of the most colorful language used to decorate everyday conversation.

In this text, we've included only the most frequently used, and therefore useful, idioms and phrasal expressions with meanings in both English and Japanese for comparison, examples for a clearer understanding and practical application of the material, and stories for added depth and practice. Literal translations were used for most definitions and sentence translations, yet for some explanations a less literal approach was taken to provide a more natural explanation in the learner's native tongue in order to keep the intention clear. The example sentences provide contextual support for more in-depth understanding of the meanings. The examples have been carefully constructed to support the definition so that in many cases, the meaning may be inferred from the example.

The stories are tailored to be accessible to learners, yet challenge them with the application of language. Following the stories are questions, designed to test the students' comprehension of the story while coaxing them to use the target language.

Finally, additional discussion questions incite deeper dialogue about the subjects raised in the story or in the use of the idioms themselves.

The chapters are organized into 25 areas of interest providing easy access to the target language. Each chapter provides opportunities for reading, writing, listening and speaking. Units can be studied in any order and, by referring to the topic and chapter headings, can provide lessons to supplement other sources.

*Idiom Attack* may be used as a classroom textbook, as a reference guide, as a supplement for other texts or for self-study. Each chapter can be studied independently of the others so that learners or teachers can easily access the subjects that most need attention. Well suited to the classroom setting or personal study, this book provides an excellent resource for a variety of applications in a user-friendly format.

Idioms are more complex than vocabulary words, but act like them in that they must fit within the grammatical structure of a sentence. Idioms can be used as all parts of speech: noun, verb, adjective or adverb. This book presents idioms in their most common form, but American idioms are a direct reflection of American culture – alive and changing. They are also dynamic in usage. For example, an idiom normally used as a noun may sometimes be used as a verb in a slightly altered form. Such forms, when common, are listed below the idiom definition with an explanation of the altered meaning. A *synonym* following the idiom explanation indicates a similar idiom with the same meaning as above, while an *antonym* indicates the opposite. Useful explanatory notes follow the idiom to explain the complexities of usage or grammar such as hyphenation of the idiom or common inclusion of words of emphasis i.e.- really, just or all. Many idioms also have dual (or more) meanings, which are represented in a cross-reference addendum at the back of the book.

Many idioms may be used interchangeably with different pronouns, such as *I, you, he, she, it, they,* etc. Thus, "one" or "someone" is used in the entry of the idiom to signify such variants. "One" or "one's" is used when the antecedent of the pronoun must refer to the subject of the sentence as in *raise one's voice, cross one's heart* or *mind one's own business*. Similarly, "someone" is used in the idiom when the antecedent of the pronoun must not refer to the grammatical subject of the sentence as in *get in someone's face* or *give someone a start*.

As the entries are arranged non-alphabetically according to each chapter's subject heading, an index is available to easily locate entries alphabetically and an additional list of idioms with dual meanings is cross-referenced for easy comparison.

Thanks for reading and please enjoy the ride. Good luck!

# Preface

序文

イディオム・アタックー二足の草鞋編は北アメリカで現在使われている慣用語300語を集めた本です。読みやすく分かりやすい構成で、学習に最適です。筋の通った多彩な題やテーマを使っているので、文脈や場面を通した学習が出来、すぐに勉強したい内容が見つかる本です。25章からなるこのテキストは中・上級者向けに作られています。しかしシンプルな英語に限定しているので、ある程度、上達した初心者をさらに伸ばす教材としてもお使い下さい。

イディオム（慣用語）とは2つ以上の単語から構成される、決まった用句です。組み合わせることで元の文字通りの意味と異なる意味を持ちます。このことから、言語特有の表現法であるイディオムは外国語を学ぶ人、または外国語を教える教師にとっても最も難しい課題でもあります。複雑ですが、日常会話を色鮮やかに飾る大切な表現法です。

このテキストでは英語を勉強する人に一番役立つ、最も頻繁に使われている慣用語を揃えています。比較出来るよう英語と日本語の意味も添えています。より深い理解や応用を目的とする例文、そして練習のためには短い物語も各章に含まれています。ほとんどの定義や例文の訳は文字通りになっていますが、それ以外にも、日本語のより自然な表現で解説を明白にするために比喩的な訳をしているところもあります。例文は文脈上の解説や意味をより深く理解するためにお使い下さい。例文は定義を裏付けるため作成されたものですので、例文から慣用語の意味を推測出来る場合も多くあります。

物語は読者にとって読みやすい内容でありながら、言葉の実用面で能力を伸ばします。ストーリーの後に続く質問は生徒の理解を確かめながら、英語を使う機会を作るためにお使い下さい。最後の質問はさらにディスカッションを誘い、それを通じてストーリーの意味の深層について話し合うことでその慣用語の使い方についても理解を深めることが出来ます。

英語への興味を誘いながら、学習しやすい25個のテーマを基に章にまとめられています。各章にリーディング、ライティング、リスニングとスピーキング力を身につける機会を設けています。順番を自由自在にアレンジ出来、テーマや章の題名を選択することで、授業の副教材に使うことも出来ます。

イディオム・アタックは授業の教科書、参考図書、副教材、または独学と使い方は多様です。各章が独立していることから、読者も教師もすぐに必要なトピックを選び出し集中的に勉強することが出来ま

す。教室の環境にも、家庭での独学にも、とても適しているこの本は、常に学ぶ人を中心にした構成で、使い方は自由自在です。

慣用語は普通の単語より意味は複雑ではあるが、普通の単語と同じように必ず文脈の文法と一体化させて使う必要があります。慣用語は名詞、動詞、副詞、形容詞のような色々な品詞の役割を果たすことがあります。この本では最も多く見られる形で紹介していますが、北アメリカ文化の反映であるイディオムはアメリカンカルチャーと同じように生き、常に変化し、使い方も進化します。例えば通常は名詞としれ使われる慣用語を少し変えて動詞として用いることがあります。常用となっている場合はこれらの使い方も解説を付けて、定義の後に紹介しています。慣用語の解説の後に「synonym」と書かれている場合は、同意語である似たような慣用語を紹介しています。これに対して「antonym」と書かれている場合は対義語を付けました。また、使い方上の注意点、ハイフンの使い方、強調のために一緒に用いる言葉（例：really, just, all）の解説も付いています。数多くの慣用語は複数の意味を持ちますので、本の後ろには相互参照のための付録が付いています。

多くの慣用語はI, you, he, she, itのような代名詞を全て入れ替えて使うことがあるので、その場合はoneまたはsomeoneを使って書いています。代名詞の先行詞が文の主語に当たる時はone, one'sを使っています（例：*raise one's voice, cross one's heart, mind one's own business*）。同様にsomeoneは代名詞の先行詞が文の主語でない場合に用いています（例：*get in someone's face, give someone a start*）。

テーマごとにまとめられている用語はアルファベット順にはなっていないので、本の後ろには簡単に用語を引けるために索引が付いています。複数の意味を持つ慣用語も相互参照できる一覧表も載っています。

このテキストが少しでも英語の勉強にお役に立てば幸いです。楽しく勉強して下さい。

Good luck!

# How to Use This Book

この本の特徴と使い方

### 1 25のテーマ別必須慣用語300語

日常生活や職場、行動をする時や感情を表現する時に必要となる、最もよく使われる慣用語が25個のテーマ別に分類されています。テーマごとに10から15個の慣用語を、例文を添えて、紹介しています。この本を通して、英会話に欠かせない300以上もの慣用語に出会います。

### 2 日本語を通して、慣用語を身に付ける

まずは日本語を通して慣用語の意味を紹介しれから、英語の例文でその使い方を見て頂きます。この勉強法でより簡単で効果的に慣用語が身に付きます。

### 3 詳細な解説で無理なく学べる

例文の慣用語の意味のニュアンスを英語で丁寧に解説しています。これに加えて日本語の定義も添えてあります。同意語、対義語、注意点や解説を使って、慣用語をさまざまな場面で使いこなして下さい。

---

**01 最初から最後まで**

## From Beginning to End

**kick off**
to start something; to officially commence something.
何かを始める；何かを正式に開催する；幕を切る。

そのチェーン全店はお祭りのような雰囲気の中で新しいセールを kick off した。
The chain of stores kicked off its new sale with a party atmosphere.

**from scratch**
from the very beginning; with no help.
最初から；何もない状態から。

リストラ後、部長は from scratch 出直さなければならなかった。
Following the layoffs, the manager had to start over from scratch.

**usher in**
to cause something new to start.
(何か新しい事を)引き起こす、もたらす、到来させる。

共産圏崩壊は予期せぬ新しい時代を usher in した。
The fall of the communist block ushered in an unexpected new era.

**finish off**
to complete something in order to bring it to an end.
何かを完全に終わらせる；何かを最後まで続ける。

彼は本を1冊 finish off すると同時に、次の一冊をすぐに始めた。
As soon as he finished one book off, he'd start another.

## 4 穴埋め問題を解いて理解を再確認

新しい例文の穴埋め問題をすることで、慣用語の意味を再確認します。例文の下に記している訳と、慣用語の一部が既にヒントとして示されていることで、簡単に慣用語全体が思い出せ、どんなに難しい慣用語でも身近なものになります。

## 5 ストーリーを読んで慣用語を文脈に沿って理解

章ごとの慣用語を使って、おもしろい内容を短くまとめたストーリーを通して、北米の人々の生活を垣間見て下さい。会話を生き生きとしたものにするべく、さまざまな場面で慣用語がどのように使われるのかを感じ取って下さい。

## 6 質問したり、質問に答えたり、話し合いに参加しながら慣用語を使いこなす

例文の慣用語の意味のニュアンスを英語で丁寧に解説しています。これに加えて日本語の定義も添えてあります。同意語、対義語、注意点や解説を使って、慣用語をさまざまな場面で使いこなして下さい。

– # Table of Contents 目次

## ❸ Taking Action 二足の草鞋

**Getting Used to Idioms** 英語慣用語に慣れよう / **4**

**Preface** 序文 / **6**

**How to Use This Book** この本の特徴と使い方 / **10**

**01. Getting Dressed** 服を着ること / **16**
try on / put on / have on / get dressed / take off / dress up go with / hand-me-down / get changed / bundle up / fold up / wear out / grow out of

**02. Staying & Going** 留まる事、行く事 / **23**
move over / head for / turn back / check out / pass by / take up / make room for / sit up straight / be right under someone's nose / on foot

**03. Commuting** 通勤 / **28**
traffic jam / rush hour / drop someone/ something off / pick up / give (someone) a ride / buckle up / on one's way / share a ride / double-park(ing) / road rage / go out of one's way

**04. Driving & Transportation** 運転と交通手段 / **34**
take a spin / go for a drive / go for a cruise / get around / get in(to) / get on(to) / get out of / get off (of) / ride shotgun / cut someone/something off / drive like crazy / make good time / tailgate / fill up / gas-guzzler / take off / set of wheels

**05. Making Plans** 計画を立てる / **42**
draw up / off the cuff / cook up / rule out / map out / up in the air / in the works / on the spur of the moment / play it by ear / wing it

## 06. Leaving 出発 / **48**
get going / be off / take off / head out / head off / hit the road / sneak off / be long gone

## 07. Celebrating Life 生きる喜び / **53**
live it up / have a ball / have a blast / live life in the fast lane / life of the party / throw a party / party animal / night on the town / paint the town red / get out and about / night owl / early bird

## 08. Health & Fitness 健康とフィットネス / **60**
get in shape / be in shape / out of shape / warm up / workout / put on weight / lay off / hit the gym / trim down / cool down / out of breath / work off / build up / catch one's breath / go on a diet

## 09. Being Aware 気付くこと / **67**
catch someone's eye / ring a bell / dawn on / look out (for) / take note (of) / pay attention (to) / stand out / take in / sink in

## 10. Aid & Advice 助けと忠告 / **72**
turn to / help someone out / rally around / pitch in / take under one's wing / words of wisdom / sound someone out / speak to / give someone a bum steer / steer someone straight

## 11. Looking For & Finding 探すこと、見つけること / **78**
go over / look up / look into / be after / find out / come up with / turn up / run across / come by / read up on

## 12. Making an Effort 努力すること / **84**
get around to / take the bull by the horns / burn the midnight oil / burn the candle at both ends / go all out / keep (it) up / halfhearted / not lift a finger / drag one's feet

## 13. Making Mistakes 間違えをする / **89**
do something over / screw up / goof up / be on the wrong track / make a mess of / mix up / put one's foot in one's mouth / mess up / faux pas / slip of the tongue / get one's wires crossed / bark up the wrong tree / not think straight

# Table of Contents

目次

### 14. Risk & Reward リスクと報酬 / **95**

be iffy / fifty-fifty / miss out (on) / chances are (that) / stand a chance / put all one's eggs in one basket / pipe dream / irons in the fire / odds are (that) / fight a losing battle / pass up / miss the boat / long shot / a sure thing

### 15. Getting Involved 参加する / **102**

show up / sit out / left out / team up (with) / look on / take part in / count someone in / count someone out / join in / have a hand in

### 16. Defense, Support & Backing 守り、援助、支援 / **108**

stand up for / come out in favor of / back up / jump on the bandwagon / ride on someone's coattails / paper trail / stand behind / not have a leg to stand on / acid test / pull for

### 17. Sweat & Determination 苦労と決意 / **113**

knuckle down / step up / get down to it / go overboard / follow something through / give it one's best shot / shoot for the moon / come on strong / get one's second wind

### 18. Wants & Needs 要望と要求 / **118**

feel like / long for / could go for / be dying for/to / have (got) dibs on / would rather / to each his own / had better / have got to / be supposed to

### 19. Inquiring & Interfering 尋ねること、干渉すること / **124**

mind one's own business / get on someone's case / get off someone's case / get lost / stick one's nose into / be none of someone's business / busybody / be in the way / knock it off

### 20. Pick & Choose 選び抜く / **1129**

pros and cons / make up one's mind / pick and choose / leave something (up) to / settle on / rule of thumb / take it or leave it / leave something open / call the shots / take one's pick

### 21. Facing Danger 危険に立ち向かう / **135**

play it safe / stick one's neck out / run the risk of / close call / touch and go / take a chance / on the line / throw caution to the wind / tread on thin ice / at stake / the chips are down / out of the woods

## 22. Clashes & Complaints 対立と不満 / **141**

have an ax to grind / rant and rave / have it out (with) / have words (with) / cause a stir / stir up a hornet's nest / nitpick / make a big deal of / harp on / blow the whistle / a bone of contention / rock the boat

## 23. Teamwork & Support チームワークとサポート / **147**

work with / play ball (with) / take turns / come together / pull together / bend over backwards / it takes two to tango / put your heads together / team up (with) / do a favor / a real sport / go out of one's way

## 24. Aptitude & Ability 才能と能力 / **153**

be all thumbs / be cut out for / be right up one's alley / have a (real) knack for / know something/someone like the back of one's hand / have a green thumb / get the hang of / lose one's touch / wet behind the ears

## 25. Memory & Loss 記憶と喪失 / **158**

forgive and forget / fade away / draw a blank / slip one's mind / pop into one's head / keep in mind / look back (on) / learn something by heart / hold on to / cry over spilled milk / be on the tip of one's tongue

**Index** インデックス / **166**

**Crossword Answers** クロスワ 霊廟飢 / **173**

# Getting Dressed

**01 服を着ること**

**try on**
to put on an item of clothing for the purpose of seeing how it looks, feels and fits.
試着する。

サイズが合うか確かめるため、ジュディーはジーンズを try on した。
Judy tried on the jeans to see if they fit.

**put on**
to cover a part of one's body with clothing.
(服などを)を着る；被る；はめる；する；履く；巻く；付ける。
*Antonym* take off.

エリックは広いつばの付いた帽子を put on して、庭作業をしに外へ行った。
Eric put on a wide-brimmed hat and went outside to work in the garden.

**have on**
to be wearing an item of clothing that is covering part of one's body.
(服などを)着ている；被っている；はめている；している；履いている；巻いている；付けている。

公共の海水浴場で泳ぐには、水着を have on することが必要だ。
It is necessary to have on a bathing suit to swim at a public beach.

**get dressed**
to put on clothes.
服を着る。

シャワーの後、私は get dressed してすぐに、仕事へ行く。
After my shower, I get dressed and go straight to work.

...ove clothing.
...を脱ぐ。
*Antonym put on.

その日はあまりにも暖かかったので、フランクはジャケットを take off した。
It was such a warm day that Frank took off his jacket.

**dress up**
to wear more formal clothes than one usually wears.
おしゃれをする；普段よりフォーマルな服を着る；正装をする。

結婚式のため、クリスタは紺のスーツで dress up した。
Christa dressed up in a navy suit for the wedding.

**go with**
to match well with something.
(色やデザインが)よく合う。
*Antonym don't go with.

緑は青とよく go with する。
Green often goes well with blue.
*Adjectives like, 'great' and 'well' are often included in the idiom.
('great'、'well'のような形容詞もよくこの慣用句に加えられます。)

**hand-me-down**
an item of clothing that was worn by an older family member or friend and is given to a younger person to wear.
お下がりの服。

家族の末っ子だったため、マシューは、小さい時、たくさんの hand-me-down をもらって着ていた。
Being the youngest person in the family, Matthew was given lots of hand-me-downs to wear when he was young.

**get changed**
to put on different items of clothing than what one is currently wearing.
着替える。

仕事から家に帰ってくると、ティムはラフな服装に get changed した。
Tim got changed into casual clothes when he came home from work.

**bundle up**
to wrap several layers of clothing around one's body in order to keep warm.
暖かいように服をたくさん着込む。

外は結構寒かったので、ブライアンが私の家を出た時、彼に bundle up するように言った。
When Brian left my house, I told him to bundle up because it was quite cold outside.

**fold up**
to neatly fold clothing before placing it somewhere.
畳む；折り畳む。

タイラーはズボンをスーツケースに入れるために fold up した。
Tyler folded up his slacks to put in the suitcase.

**wear out**

to use (by wearing) an item of clothing until it is no longer wearable.
服をボロボロになるまで着る；着つぶす。

**grow out of**

to no longer be able to wear an item of clothing because the person has grown larger.
大きくなって、服が着られなくなる。

私の子供達は服が小さくなる前に、それをよく wear out していた。とてもお金が掛かった。
My children often wore out their clothes before they actually grew out of them. It was very expensive.

エニックは3ヶ月でジーンズが grow out of した。
Ennik grew out of her jeans in three months.

# Fill in the blanks with the appropriate idioms.

**01** Since Bruce was the youngest of four boys, most of his clothes were _____ - _____ - _____ from his older siblings.
4人兄弟の末っ子だったため、ブルースの服のほとんどは兄達からのお下がりだった。

**02** Todd could hear the winter wind howling outside, so he knew he needed to _____ _____ his winter coat.
戸外で冬の風がうなっているのが聞こえていたので、トッドは冬のコートを着ないといけないと知っていた。

**03** While trying on clothes, Joan tried to get _____ as fast as she could so she could get to the next store before it closed.
服の試着をしている時、ジョーンは次の店が閉店する前にその店に行けるように、出来るだけ早く着替えようとした。

**04** Each morning Ruth had to help her young daughter _____ _____ for school.
毎朝幼い娘が学校へ行くために服を着るのを、ルースは手伝わなければいけなかった。

**05** Pete was embarrassed that he _____ _____ the same shirt as his friend at the rooftop barbeque party.
ピートは、屋上バーベキューで友達と同じシャツを着ていることを恥ずかしく思った。

**06** Amanda had to _____ on every pair of shoes before she decided which ones to purchase.
アマンダは先に全ての靴を試着してからでないとどれを購入するかを決められなかった。

**07** The snow was drifting across the road and icicles were forming next to the window, so Floyd knew he needed to _____ _____ before heading out in the cold weather.
路上に雪が吹いて、窓のそばにつららが出来てきていたので、この寒い天候の中を出掛けるには、服を着込まないといけないとフロイドは知っていた。

**08** Mom wanted both boys to _____ _____ because their grandparents were coming over for dinner.
祖父母が夕食に家に来るので、お母さんは息子2人に、普段よりフォーマルな服装をして欲しいと思っていた。

**09** Over the summer holiday, Mitchell _____ out _____ most of his pants as he gained a lot of extra weight.
夏休みの間に、ミッチェルは体重が非常に増えたので、ほとんどのズボンが着られなくなった。

**10** Being three years old, Ali isn't quite sure which shirts _____ _____ which pants.

アリは3歳だから、どのシャツがどのズボンに合うのか、ちゃんと分かっていない。

**11** Tara knew that her son would _____ _____ his favorite shoes in a few months so she encouraged him to play on the grass barefoot.

数ヶ月の間で、息子が一番お気に入りの靴をボロボロにすると分かっていたので、ターラは、芝生の上では裸足で遊ぶように、仕向けた。

**12** The heat was beginning to get unbearable, so Zak decided to _____ off his shirt.

耐えがたい暑さになり始めたので、ザックはシャツを脱ぐことにした。

**13** Bradley knew that he should _____ up his T-shirts to make more room in his dresser.

Tシャツを畳んで、タンスにもっと場所を作るべきだとブラドリーは分かっていた。

**Answers** 1. hand–me-downs  2. put on  3. (get) changed  4. get dressed  5. had on  6. try (on)  7. bundle up  8. dress up  9. grew (out) of  10. go with  11. wear out  12. take (off)  13. fold (up)

# Read the following story and refer to the questions below.

### - Fringe Benefits

Simon loved working at the Zap clothing store. He never had to dress up for work. He really liked having an unlimited* amount of in-style clothes to put on each morning when he got dressed.

This season, the stores were full of scarves for people to bundle up with. Simon had grown up as the youngest of five boys in a modest household*. As a child, he would have to wait until his older siblings would grow out of their clothes before he would get their hand-me-downs. Quite often some of the nicest items were completely worn out before they got to him. But now, since he worked at the Zap and all employees had to have on Zap clothing at work, Simon always had new clothes. He enjoyed trying on new Zap clothes and buying them using his employee discount.

Simon's job was quite easy. For most of the day he would fold up pants and sweaters that customers had picked up. He was good at helping people decide which tops go with which bottoms. His least favorite part of the job was working at the back of the store, where all he had to do was show people where to get changed and then pick the clothes off the floor that they had taken off.

*unlimited 無限；限りない   *modest household 質素な家庭

## Questions about the story

1. What does Simon like about getting dressed for work?
2. What were the stores full of this season? What are people doing?
3. When would Simon receive hand-me-downs from his older brothers?
4. In what condition were his hand-me-downs most of the time?
5. What kind of clothes was he required to have on while working?
6. What does he do most of the day?
7. What does Simon least like to do when he is working?

## Questions for discussion

1. When you were younger, did you receive many hand-me-downs? How did you feel about it?
2. What do you wear to bundle up in the morning?
3. Do you wear out your clothes quickly? Why?
4. What do you have on now? Do the clothes go well together?
5. How long does it usually take you to get dressed in the morning?
6. Do you fold up all of your clothes and put them away when you have taken them off?
7. If you were going to bundle up for the cold weather, what would you put on?

### 店員の特権

サイモンはZap洋服店で働くのが大好きだった。仕事のために正装をしないといけないことは今までなかった。毎朝服を着る時に、流行の服が好きなだけ着られるのがとても良かった。

今の季節、客が着込めるスカーフがたくさん店に並んでいた。サイモンは、質素な家庭の5人兄弟の末っ子として育った。子供の時は、兄達が大きくなって、着られなくなった服がお下がりでもらえるのを待たないといけなかった。一番良い服の多くは彼の所に届くまでによくボロボロになってしまった。しかし、Zapの従業員は皆仕事中、Zapの服を着ないといけないので、今では、Zapで働いているおかげで、サイモンはいつも新しい服を持っていた。Zapの新しい服を試着して、社員割引を使って買うのが楽しかった。

サイモンの仕事は結構、簡単だった。一日の大半は客が手に取ったズボンやセーターを畳んでいた。どの上下が合うか客が決めるのを手伝ってあげるのが得意だった。一番苦手な仕事は、店の奥の試着室へ客を案内して、床に脱ぎ捨てられた服を拾うことだった。

# Staying & Going 02

留まる事、行く事

**move over**
to change one's position to either the left or the right, usually to create room.
(場所を空けるために)寄る、横へ移る、ずれる。

バスで、お母さんとその子供のために場所を空けるため、男性は move over した。
On the bus, a man moved over to make room for a mother and her child.

**head for**
to move or travel in a particular direction.
どこかへ向かう、直進する。

4時間の旅の後、ドリューは空港のお手洗いへ head for した。
After four hours of traveling, Drew headed for the airport washroom.

**turn back**
to change one's direction towards the place of origin; to return.
折り返えす；戻る；180度方向転換をする。

嵐で橋が流されてしまったので、クリスタは turn back しなといけなかった。
Christa had to turn back because the bridge had been washed out in the storm.

**check out**
to sign out and leave a place (usually a hotel or hospital, where you sign in and stay for a period of time), or to end your involvement with an activity or situation.
チェックアウトする；退院する；手続きを済ませて出て行く；(状態から、参加していたことから)抜け出す。

他の患者が痛がって叫んでいるのが聞こえた途端、サンディーは自分で病院から check out した。
Sandy checked out of the hospital as soon as she heard other patients scream in pain.

**pass by**
to go past a person or place without stopping.
(人、または場所を)止まらずに通りすぎる。
*Noun* passer-by.
通行人、通りがかりの人。

ジェーンは事故現場を pass by することにした。
Jane decided to pass by the accident scene.

**take up**
to occupy space or time.
(場所または時間を)取る。

サムはあまりにも大きかったので、公園のベンチの2人分の場所を take up した。
Sam was so big that he took up the space of two people on the park bench.

**make room for**
to make space for someone or something.
(誰か、何かのために)場所を空ける。

ジェイクは大きいので、ケビンは車の中で彼のために make room for しないといけなかった。
Since Jake is a big guy, Kevin needed to make room for him in the car.

**sit up straight**
to sit with one's back upright and in an erect position.
背筋を伸ばして座る。

コーチはチーム全員へ sit up straight して集中するようにお願いした。
The coach implored his team to sit up straight and pay attention.

**be right under someone's nose**
in plain view; to be directly in front of, or extremely close to someone and in an easy to identify, obvious place.
目の前にいる；すぐそばにいる；すぐ目のつくところにいる。

お母さんが料理をしていると、愛犬はいつも be right under her nose だ。
When mom is cooking, the family dog is always right under her nose.

**on foot**
walking.
徒歩で；歩いて。
*Synonym* by foot.

私の家まで遠くないので、私達は on foot で行ける。
It's not far to my house, so we can go on foot.

# Fill in the blanks with the appropriate idioms.

**01** Pauline decided to _____ _____ of the situation before it got any worse and escalated into a fight.

事態が悪化して喧嘩に発展する前にポーリンは抜け出すことにした。

**02.** Raymond's mother always reminded him to _____ up _____ at the supper table.

レイモンドは夕食時の食卓では背筋をちゃんと伸ばして座るようにと、母親にいつも注意されていた。

**03** The police were embarrassed when they found out the criminal was _____ their _____ the entire time.

初めからずっと犯罪者が目の前にいたのを知って、警察は当惑した。

**04** Once Susan invited her brother to stay over for a few days, she and her husband had to do some cleaning and _____ room _____ him in the spare bedroom.

家に何日か泊まりにくるように弟を誘った後、スーザンと夫は掃除をして、彼のための寝室を用意しなければいけなかった。

**05** The usher asked the audience members on the end of the aisles to move _____ to let a young group of moviegoers sit together.

映画を見に来た若者の集団が一緒に座れるように、案内係は列の端にいた観客に席をずれるようにお願いした。

**06** The scouts were not happy once they found out they were going to have to go to the new campsite _____ _____.

新しいキャンプ場へ歩いていかないといけないと知った時からボーイスカウト達は不機嫌だった。

**07** The airline charges large people for two seats when they _____ up too much space.

体が大きいために場所をとり過ぎる客に、その航空会社は2座席分の航空料金を払わせている。

**08** Abigail had to tuck her feet under her chair to let others _____ by and get to their seats.

他の客が通って席まで着けるように、アビゲールは足を椅子のしたに引っ込めないといけなかった。

**09** Just before intermission, Dillon decided to _____ _____ the washroom.

幕間の直前にディロンはお手洗いへ向かうことにした。

**10** Once the cold wind began to sting his face, Alan decided to _____ back and go home.

冷たい風で顔がヒリヒリし始めた時、アランは折り返して家に帰ることにした。

**Answers** 1. check out  2. sit (up) straight  3. right under (their) noses  4. make (room) for  5. (move) over  6. on foot  7. take (up)  8. pass (by)  9. head for  10. turn (back)

# Read the following story and refer to the questions below.

### - Opening Night

Opening night was here and Steven had never been more excited. It was his debut and he had invited most of his family and friends. He realized his reserved seats would take up at least two rows of the theater. He asked the ushers to do their best to make room for his guests. While the ushers were busy inside the theater having people move over to keep pairs of seats open, outside parking was a mess.

Steven had told his family to arrive early because of the traffic around the theater. The show had received a lot of, press and they would likely have to turn back people at the door if they arrived late. Since they lived only nine blocks from downtown, many of Steven's family decided to travel on foot to the premiere*.

The weather was a little chilly, so as soon as they arrived, they headed for the bar for a hot Irish coffee*. Steven's younger sister passed by the bar to look at the programs and gift counter. She knew she would have to check out early to get to work on time, but she wanted to have a T-shirt with her brother's picture on it. Steven stood near the counter searching the crowd for his family. While he scanned, he didn't even realize that his sister was right under his nose the whole time. Once his sister stood up and he found the rest of his family, they took their seats. Steven felt like a celebrity*, so he sat up straight and grinned from ear to ear.

*premiere* プレミア；(映画や劇の)初演　*Irish coffee* アイリッシュ・コーヒー(熱いコーヒーにウィスキーを加え、生クリームを乗せたもの。)　*celebrity* 有名人；アイドル

## Questions about the story

1. How much space would the reserved seats occupy?
2. What did Steven ask the ushers to do?
3. What were the ushers doing?
4. Why might the theater have to turn people back?
5. How did Steven's family arrive at the theater?
6. What did Steven's family head for after they arrived at the theater and why?
7. Where was Steven's sister sitting?

## Questions for discussion

1. When you are riding on public transportation, do you make room for pregnant women or the elderly?
2. Do you tend to sit up straight or do you slouch in your chair?
3. How far do you usually go on foot daily?
4. What are some hard-to-find items that usually end up right under one's nose?
5. When driving, do you tend to pick up hitchhikers or just pass them by?
6. Where are you headed after this class?

### 初演の夜

初演の夜が訪れて、スティーブンは今までで一番ワクワクしていた。これは彼のデビューだったので、家族と友達をほぼ全員呼んでいた。彼が予約した席が少なくとも映画館の席のうち、2列を埋めてしまうことに気付いた。案内係に、彼が呼んだ客のために出来るだけ場所をつくるようにお願いした。すべての案内係が、館内でペア席を作るために観客に寄ってもらっている間、外の駐車場は大混乱になっていた。

映画館周辺の渋滞のことを考えて、スティーブンは家族に早く来るように言っていた。映画はマスコミから注目を浴びていたので、遅れてくる人はきっと追い返されることになっただろう。スティーブンの家族は都心部から9ブロックしか離れていない所に住んでいたので、彼らのほとんどは歩いてプレミアに来ることにした。

空気が少し冷え込んでいたので、到着してすぐに、彼らは暖かいアイリッシュ・コーヒーを飲みにバーへ向かった。スティーブンの妹はバーを通り過ぎて、プログラムやお土産の展示を見に行った。彼女は、時間通りに仕事に行くために、早めに抜けないといけないのが分かっていたが、兄の顔が描かれているTシャツが欲しかった。スティーブンはカウンターの近くに立ち、人ごみの中にいる家族を探していた。周りを見回している間、妹がずっと目の前にいたことにスティーブンは気付いていなかった。妹が立ち上がって、残りの家族も見つかってから、彼らは席に着いた。スティーブンは有名人になった気がしたので、背筋をピーンと伸ばして、満面の笑顔を浮かべて座っていた。

# 03 通勤 Commuting

**traffic jam**
a large number of vehicles close together and unable to move or moving very slowly.
渋滞。
*Synonym* bumper-to-bumper traffic.

デモ参加者が道に出るとほとんどの場合は、traffic jam を引き起こす。
Protest demonstrations on the street usually cause a traffic jam.

**rush hour**
a period of heavy traffic in the morning or evening when people are traveling to or from work.
通勤ラッシュ；ラッシュ時。

rush hour の中に運転するのは好きではないので、通常ジュディーは早めに仕事へ行って遅くまで残業をする。
Since she doesn't like driving during rush hour, Judy usually arrives earlier and works late at the office.

**drop someone/something off**
to bring someone or something to a place and continue to travel.
誰か・何かを届けるために途中で降ろす。

明日雨が降っていたら、父が通勤途中に学校で drop me off してあげると僕に言った。
My father said that he would drop me off at school on his way to work tomorrow if it's raining.

**pick up**
to take someone or something from a place and continue to travel.
途中で誰か・何かを拾うまたは、乗せる；何かを取りに行く；誰かを迎えに行く。

仕事の後、私は家に帰る前に、クリーニングに出した服を pick up する。
After work, I pick up my dry cleaning before coming home.

### give (someone) a ride
to provide transportation to another person.
(車・バイクなどに)誰かを乗せて送る。
*Synonym give (someone) a lift.

もし月曜日までに車が直らなかったら私が会社まであなたを give a ride するわ。
If you can't get your car fixed before Monday, I will give you a ride to work.

### buckle up
to put on or fasten the safety belt that keeps one in one's seat in case of an accident.
シートベルトをする。

家族全員が buckle up しているかどうか確かめてからでないと父は家の私道から絶対に出ない。
My father never leaves the driveway without ensuring that our family is buckled up.

### on one's way
in the direction that one is traveling.
行く途中である；向かっている方向である；(目的地へ)向かう。

お別れを言いに祖父母の所まで運転して行ってから、ジミーは大学へ on his way した。
After driving to his grandparents to say goodbye, Jimmy was on his way to college.

### share a ride
for several people to commute using one vehicle.
数人が同じ車で移動、または通勤・通学をする；相乗りをする。
*Synonym carpool; rideshare.

ガソリン代を節約するため、3人の男性は仕事の往復を毎日 share a ride する。
To save money on gas, the three men all share a ride to and from work each day.

### double-park(ing)
to park illegally next to a legally parked vehicle on the roadway.
車を二重に駐車する違法行為。

他の車の横に駐車をしたせいで車両の通行を妨げたクリスは double-parking 違反カードを渡された。
After parking beside another car and blocking traffic, Chris received a ticket for double-parking.

### road rage
uncontrollable anger due to the stress of traffic conditions.
ドライバー激怒症(追い越しなど他のドライバーのささいな行為に攻撃的・暴力的な反応を示す)。

仕事場での長い一日の後、渋滞の中にいるとチャックは簡単に road rage になる。
After a long day at work, Chuck gets road rage easily in heavy traffic.

**go out of one's way**
to go somewhere not in the direction that one is traveling.
遠回りをする；回り道をする。

友達は車を持っていないので、私は仕事の後に彼を家まで送るため毎日 **go out of my way** する。

I **go out of my way** every day to drive my friend home after work because he doesn't have a car.

# Fill in the blanks with the appropriate idioms.

**01** On the way home from school, Mom stopped at the cleaners to _____ off Dad's shirts.

学校から家へ帰る途中にお母さんは、お父さんのシャツを届けるためクリーニング店に立ち寄った。

**02** In Dalton's new car, the driver has to _____ _____ before the car will start.

ダルトンの新車では、運転手がシートベルトをしないと車はスタートできない。

**03** George could not find a parking spot in front of his apartment building so he decided to _____ - _____ alongside another car.

自分のマンションの前にスペースを見つけられなかったので、ジョージは他の車の隣に二重駐車をすることにした。

**04** Frank and Linda decided to leave early to avoid the _____ _____ traffic between **7** am and **8** am in the city.

フランクとリンダは市内の７時から８時までの通勤ラッシュを避けるために、早めに出発することにした。

**05** Bob decided to drive his coworker home because it was _____ his _____ home.

家に帰る途中に同僚の家があったので、ボブは彼を送ることにした。

**06** Since they were both going to the same conference in the city, Bob and Doug decided to _____ a _____ to save on expenses.

２人とも同じ町にある会議へ行く予定だったため、ボブとダグは経費を節約するために、相乗りして行くことにした。

**07** The construction caused the road to be narrowed to one lane, so naturally there was a _____ _____ during rush hour.

道路工事で車線は１つに減っていたので、当然ラッシュ時には渋滞が発生した。

**08** On the way home, Tom's air conditioning stopped working and another vehicle almost collided with his car. He had to take several deep breaths to calm himself down so he would not get _____ rage.

家へ帰る途中に、トムの車のエアコンが故障して、その上に他の車が危うく衝突して来そうになった。彼はドライバー激怒症にならないように、深呼吸をして、自分を落ち着かせないといけなかった。

**09** Dad decided to give _____ _____ to the man walking on the side of the road because it was very hot.

とても暑かったので、お父さんは道の脇を歩いていた人を乗せてあげることにした。

Commuting

**10** When Dad stopped the car to _____ _____ the man, he realized that it was an old friend from college.
男性を乗せるためにお父さんが車を停めた時、その男性は大学時代の旧友だと気付いた。

**11** Dad asked where his old friend was headed and chose to go _____ _____ his _____ to take him there.
お父さんは旧友にどこまで行くのかを聞いて、回り道をしてそこまで送ることにした。

**Answers**  1. drop (off)  2. buckle up  3. double-park  4. rush hour  5. on (his) way  6. share (a) ride  7. traffic jam  8. road (rage)  9. (give) a ride  10. pick up  11. out of (his) way

# Read the following story and refer to the questions below.

### - Saving Gas

Hank was thrilled about his new job in the city. It was quite far from his house, but he hoped to be able to **share a ride** with someone from work. Hank was **on his way** early because he wanted to avoid the **rush hour**. Last week he had heard on the radio that there had been a huge **traffic jam**. He also heard about one man who got **road rage** in the heat when another vehicle nearly collided with his, so he wanted to stay away from the traffic jam if he could.

At work, Hank put up a sign on the message board stating that he would be willing to **give a ride** to people from the suburbs\* if they would share in the cost of the gas. By the end of his first day, Hank had received four emails from people saying they wanted him to **pick them up** in the morning. Three of Hank's coworkers lived **on his way to work** and the fourth person did not. He would have to go **out of his way** to pick her up, but she would help with the gas, so Hank decided it was worthwhile to get her. The woman lived in an apartment building, and Hank knew he would have to **double-park** each morning while he waited for her.

After work, all five of them got into Hank's car so he could **drop them off on his way** home. Since Hank knew safety was important, he told everyone to **buckle up** and then they could **be on their way**.

*suburb 郊外；(大都市を通勤範囲とする)市、町、村、近郊住宅地域

## Questions about the story

1. How did Hank hope to get to work every day?
2. Why did he leave for work early?
3. What was he trying to avoid by going to work early?
4. What two things did Hank hear on the radio?
5. What did the sign on the message board say that he would be willing to do?
6. Were all of the people who wanted to share a ride on his way to work?
7. How would he have to park to pick up one of his coworkers?
8. What did Hank have everyone do every time they got into his car?

## Questions for discussion

1. Have you ever participated in a ridesharing program?
2. What time are the morning and evening rush hours in your country? How long do they last?
3. What is the fine if you are caught driving without buckling up?
4. Do you ever get road rage? How do you calm yourself down?
5. Do you ever go out of your way to pick up or drop off people or things as a favor for somebody?
6. How can someone avoid getting stuck in a traffic jam?
7. If you are caught in a traffic jam, what are some things that you can do to pass the time?
8. What is the single busiest day to drive each year?

### ガソリンの節約

都会での新しい仕事が始まるのでハンクはとても喜んでいた。家からかなり遠かったが、仕事仲間の誰かと一緒に相乗りができればいいと思っていた。通勤ラッシュを避けたかったので、ハンクは早めに仕事へ向かっていた。先週、ラジオで大きな渋滞があったと聞いていた。しかも、他の車と衝突しそうになってドライバー激怒症になった男性の話も聞いていたので、できる限り渋滞を避けたいと思っていた。

会社の掲示板にハンクは、ガソリン代を割り勘にして郊外に住んでいる人の送り迎えの提供をしたいと言うメッセージを載せた。初日が終わった時点で、朝に乗せて欲しいと言うメールが4人から来ていた。同僚の3人は彼の通勤ルートの途中に住んでいたが、4人目はそうではなかった。彼女を拾うためには、遠回りをしないといけないが、彼女がその分のガソリン代を出してくれるから、行く甲斐はあるとハンクは決めた。

女性はマンションに住んでいたので、彼女を待っている間は毎朝、二重駐車をしないといけないことをハンクは知っていた。仕事が終わった後、帰宅途中に降ろしてあげられるように、ハンクの車に5人乗り込んだ。ハンクは安全を第一に考えていたので、出発する前に、皆にシートベルトをするように言った。

# 04 Driving & Transportation
運転と交通手段

**take a spin**
to go for a short enjoyable drive.
車の一乗り；短いドライブ。

トッドの友達は皆、彼の新しいバイクで take a spin したいと思った。
All of Todd's friends wanted to take a spin on his new motorcycle.

**go for a drive**
to take a trip in a vehicle for pleasure.
ドライブをする。

私は日曜日に、田舎へ go for a drive するのが好きだ。
On Sundays, I like to go for a drive out to the country.
*To 'go for a drive' is considered to be more formal and to take much longer than 'take a spin'.
('go for a drive'は'take a spin'より長くて堅苦しいものです。)

**go for a cruise**
to take a pleasurable ride or trip in a vehicle for usually a farther distance than to 'go for a drive' or 'take a spin'.
('go for a drive' や 'take a spin'よりも長い)ドライブをする。

私は日曜日に、大きい車を出して家族で田舎へ go for a cruise する時が一番好きだ。
On Sundays, I like it best when our family takes the big car out and we go for a cruise around the countryside.

## get around
to travel to and from various places.
さまざまな所へ移動する；自由に移動する。

町の中を get around するために私はスクーターが必要だった。
I needed a scooter so that I could get around town.

## get in(to)
to board or to enter a vehicle by sitting down.
自動車に乗る；乗車する。
*Synonym* hop in.

若い学生はタクシーに get in して、運転手に出来るだけ早く学校へ行くように言った。
The young student got in the taxi and told the driver to go to the school as quick as he could.

## get on(to)
to board or to enter a vehicle by walking.
乗り物に乗る、乗車する。
*Synonym* hop on(to).

船に get on するには、ドックからジャンプしなければいけない。
To get on the boat, we need to jump from the dock.
*People get on of buses, trains, boats, motorcycles, bicycles and airplanes.
(バス、電車、船、バイク、自転車、飛行機に 'get on' すると言います。)

## get out of
to leave or to exit a vehicle in which one must sit.
(車から)降りる。
*Also* hop out (of).

私は車から get out of して、学校へ歩いた。
I got out of the car and walked to school.
*This is only used for automobiles.
(この表現は自動車の時にしか使いません。)

## get off (of)
to leave or to exit a vehicle.
(乗り物)から降りる。
*Synonym* hop off (of).

携帯が鳴っていたため、次の駅でバイオレットは地下鉄を get off しなければいけなかった。
Violet had to get off the subway at the next stop because her cell phone was ringing.
*People get off of buses, trains, boats, motorcycles, bicycles and airplanes.
(バス、電車、船、バイク、自転車、飛行機から 'get off' すると言います。)

## ride shotgun
to ride in the front passenger seat.
前の席に乗る；助手席に乗る。

田舎へドライブに行くなら、私は ride shotgun したい。
If you are going for a country drive, I want to ride shotgun.

### cut someone/something off
to drive in the direct path of another driver at close range.
道路をさえぎる；他の車の前に急に飛び出る。

若い運転手は間違えてcut another car offして、高速道路で大きな交通事故を引き起こしてしまった。
The young driver mistakenly cut another car off and caused a serious traffic accident on the highway.

### drive like crazy
to drive as if one is insane or to drive extremely unsafely.
暴走する；かなり飛ばして運転する；危険な運転をする。
*Synonym* drive like a maniac.

時間通りここに着くために私はdrive like crazyした。
I drove like crazy just to get here in time.
*Usually without regard for other people or property.
(通常、他人や周りも気を付けずに運転する時にこの慣用句を使います。)

### make good time
to travel a distance in a shorter than expected time.
予定より速く移動する。

町への道のりで私は本当にmake good timeした。そこに着くまでにいつもの4時間に比べて、3時間しか掛からなかった。
I really made good time on my trip to the city. It only took me three hours instead of the regular four hours to get there.
*Adjectives such as 'bad', 'terrible', 'excellent' and 'great' may replace 'good'.
'good' の代わりに'bad', 'terrible', 'excellent', 'great' のような形容詞を使うこともあります。

### tailgate
to follow too closely to the car directly in front.
前の車のすぐ後ろを運転する。

バスはよくtailgateするので、私の母はバスの前を走るのは好きではない。
My mother doesn't like driving in front of buses because they usually tailgate.

### fill up
to put as much fuel as possible in a gas tank.
満タンにする。

兄の車をfill upするのは本当に嫌いだ。とても大きなガソリンタンクとシリンダが8個もある。
I really dislike filling up my brother's car. It has eight cylinders and a very large gas tank.

**gas-guzzler**
a vehicle that consumes large amounts of fuel.
ガソリン消費量の多い大型自動車。
***Synonym** gas-hog.

**take off**
to leave in a rush or hurry.
急いで行く；急いで去る。
***Synonym** have to fly.

**set of wheels**
one's transportation (usually a car).
自分が移動できるための車・バイク。
***Synonym** wheels

私が小さかった頃、大人は皆 gas-guzzler を運転していたのを覚えている。
I remember when I was young; all of the adults drove large gas-guzzlers.

上司から電話が掛かってきた時、ジョーは緊急会議に参加するため会社へ take off しなければならなかった。
When his boss called, Joe had to take off for the office to attend an urgent meeting.

良い set of wheels が買えるように私はお金を貯めている。
I am saving some money so that I can buy a nice set of wheels.

# Fill in the blanks with the appropriate idioms.

**01** James did not look as he was changing lanes and mistakenly _____ someone _____.
確認せずに車線を変えたので、ジェームズは間違えて誰かの前に飛び出してしまった。

**02** They had a long drive ahead of them, so Frank and Sue left early to avoid the rush hour traffic and _____ _____ _____ on the way to the resort.
リゾートまで長い道のりだったので、ラッシュを避けるため、フランクとスーは早めに出発することにし、リゾートまで速く運転した。

**03** Ron was looking to buy an inexpensive little car for his son to _____ _____ in while he was attending university.
ロンは息子の大学在学中の移動のために、安くて小さい車を買いたかったので、探していた。

**04** Al was waiting for the price of gasoline to drop so he could _____ _____ his car for the trip.
ガソリンの値段が下がってから、旅行のためにタンクを満タンにしようとアルは待っていた。

**05** As the group of young men left the club, they began to run for the car because they all wanted to ride _____.
クラブから出てきた途端、若者の男性グループは皆、車の助手席に乗りたかったため走り出した。

**06** When Chris drove his new car to school, all of his friends wanted to _____ a _____ around town in it.
クリスが新しい車を運転して通学した時、友達は皆それに乗って町を一周したがっていた。

**07** During his driving test, Randal knew he should not _____ and should stay a safe distance away from the car in front of him.
運転免許取得のテスト時、ランダルは前の車と安全な間隔を保って、すぐ後ろを走らない方がいいと分かっていた。

**08** Dad always said that to save money, I should buy a car that is good on gas not one that is a _____-_____.
お金を節約するなら、ガソリンをたくさん使う大型車よりガソリン効率が良い車を選んだ方が良いと、お父さんはいつも言っていた。

**09** When the plane arrives at the airport, the people flying first class usually _____ _____ of the airplane before any of the other passengers.
飛行機が空港に到着すると、通常はファーストクラスの乗客が他の乗客より先に飛行機から降りる。

**10** It took a few minutes for the whole family to _____ _____ the van with all of the luggage packed inside.

全員の荷物でいっぱいの車に家族が皆乗るには数分掛かった。

**11** Mom pulled up to the front of the school so the children could _____ out _____ the car and go to class.

子供達が車を降りて教室へ行けるように、お母さんは学校の前に車を停めた。

**12** Burt was excited about his new _____ _____ _____ and could not wait to pick up his girlfriend in it.

新しい車にバートはワクワクしていて、彼女を迎えに行くのが待ちきれなかった。

**13** Sally loved Burt's new car and wanted to go _____ a _____ in the country.

サリーはバートの新車が大好きで、田舎へドライブに行きたがっていた。

**14** He was already **10** minutes late for the interview, so Billy had to _____ _____ _____ to get there on time.

面接へ行くのにもうすでに10分遅れていたので、時間通り到着するにはビリーはかなり飛ばして運転しないといけなかった。

**15** When Zack drove up to Jessica's house on a motorcycle and handed her a helmet, she was a little afraid to _____ on it.

ザックがバイクに乗ってジェシカの家の前に来てヘルメットを差し出した時、彼女はバイクに乗るのを少し怖がった。

**16** Norman finished his paperwork quickly on Friday afternoon so he could _____ _____ early for his weekend ski trip.

金曜日の午後、ノーマンは週末のスキー旅行へ早めに出発できるように、書類の整理を急いで終わらせた。

**17** Tim and Alex both rented jet skis and went for _____ _____ while on vacation.

旅行中にティムもアレックスもジェットスキーを借りて乗り回した。

**Answers** 1. cut (someone) off  2. made good time  3. get around  4. fill up  5. (ride) shotgun  6. take (a) spin  7. tailgate  8. gas-guzzler  9. get off (of)  10. get in  11. get (out) of  12. set of wheels  13. (go) for (a) drive  14. drive like crazy  15. get (on)  16. take off  17. (went for) a cruise

# Read the following story and refer to the questions below.

### - Car Shopping

Colin worked hard all summer long to save enough money to buy a car. He was leaving home for university in September and he needed a set of wheels to get around in. Colin asked his older brother Troy to help him find a car. Troy agreed to go for a drive around the city looking for some affordable and dependable transportation. Troy said that while they were in his car, Colin would have to ride shotgun, but when they took other cars out, Colin could drive.

Colin had used the newspaper to find some cars that he was interested in taking for a spin. Since he had mapped out* their route through the city the night before, he and Troy would make good time going from one car lot to another. Colin and Troy stopped to fill up Troy's car before they got going. Troy told Colin that since fuel was so expensive, Colin should not even look at any gas-guzzlers. Troy had Colin go in and pay while he pumped the gas* because he was in a hurry. He had plans later that afternoon and wanted to take off as soon as they were done.

Troy finished pumping the gas and waited for Colin to come back from paying and get into the car. When he pulled out of the gas station, Troy did not look carefully enough and mistakenly cut someone off. The driver of the other car was visibly* upset, so Troy drove like crazy to get further ahead of him. The other car pulled up behind Troy and continued to tailgate them. Colin suggested that Troy pull over to the side and let the other driver pass by them.

All Colin had wanted to do was go for a cruise around the city and look at cars. Now all he wanted to do was to get out of this car and avoid any problems they might have with the other driver. Colin thought that maybe a better idea would have been to buy a day pass and get onto a city bus instead of going with Troy. That way, he could get off of the bus at each car lot and not have to worry about bothering his brother.

\***map out** (場所や物)を精密に地図(図)に示す　\***pump the gas** ガソリンを入れる
\***visibly** 目に見える；明らかに

## Questions about the story

1. Why did Colin work hard all summer long?
2. Why was he leaving home?
3. Where did he ride when he was in Troy's car?
4. What kind of car was Colin looking for?
5. What happened after Troy cut off another driver?
6. What was the only thing that Collin wanted to do in the city?
7. Why did Troy tell Colin to pump the gas?
8. What does Colin think of Troy's driving?

## Questions for discussion

1. Do you prefer driving or riding shotgun when you go for a drive?
2. What are some ways to make good time when traveling?
3. What type of car would you consider to be a gas-guzzler in your country?
4. How much does it cost to fill up your car?
5. Have you ever driven like crazy? If so, when and why?
6. Have you ever cut someone off while driving?
   Did you do it on purpose?

### 車のショッピング

コリンは車を買うお金を貯めるために夏中一生懸命働いた。9月から大学へ通うために家を出るので、移動するための車が必要だった。車を探すのを兄のトロイに手伝ってもらえるか頼んだ。トロイは市内をドライブして、安くて信頼性のある車を探しに行ってもいいと賛成した。トロイの車に乗っている間はコリンが助手席に座らないといけないが、他の車を試し乗りする時はコリンが運転してもいいとトロイは言った。

コリンは試し乗りしたいと思う車を新聞で見つけていた。前の晩に市内を移動するルートを地図に書いていたので、中古車置場から中古車置場への移動が早くできると思っていた。行く前にトロイの車のガソリンを満タンにするために、二人は停まった。ガソリンがあまりにも高いから、消費量の高い大型車は見る必要もないとトロイはコリンに言った。トロイは急いでいたので彼がガソリンを入れている間、コリンにお金を払いに行かせた。トロイは午後過ぎに予定があったので、終わったらすぐに急いで出掛けたかった。

トロイはガソリンを入れ終えて、コリンが支払いから戻ってきて車に乗るのを待っていた。ガソリンスタンドから出て来た時、ちゃんと注意して見なかったので、誤って他人の車の前を遮ってしまった。その車の運転手は見るからに怒っていたので、トロイは逃ようとして、スピードを出して飛ばした。その車はトロイの後ろへ出てきて間隔をほとんど開けずにすぐ後方を走り続けた。コリンはトロイに車を道路の脇に寄せて、その運転手を通らせてあげたらいいと言った。

コリンはただ車を見回って市内をドライブしたかっただけだったのに。今ではその車の運転手とのもめ事を避けるために、ただ車から降りたいと思っていた。トロイと一緒に行くより、一日乗車券を買って市バスに乗った方が良かったかもしれないとコリンは思った。そうすれば兄に迷惑を掛けるのを気にしないでそれぞれの中古車置場で降りられたのに。

# 05 Making Plans

計画を立てる

**draw up**
to create an organized plan; to put in writing.
(計画)を練る；(文書、リストを)作成する。

デボンはお城の包囲攻撃のための計画を draw up すると決めた。
Devon decided to draw up plans for a siege of the castle.
*Usually used for more detailed or formal plans.
(通常は詳細な、または正式な企画を作る時に使います。)

**off the cuff**
impromptu or spontaneously; without preparation.
即座に・即座の；とっさに；準備も練習もせずに。

マットは off the cuff で仕事が出来るような人ではない。なんでも計画を立てるのが好きな人だ。
Matt isn't the kind of guy who can work off the cuff. He likes to plan everything.

**cook up**
to invent a story, plan, etc., usually dishonestly.
(話・弁解を)でっち上げる、ごまかす；(計画を)秘密に作る；物語を作る。

サムは夏休みの間に少し余計にお金を稼ぐために、おもしろい計画を cook up した。
Sam cooked up an interesting plan to earn some extra money during summer vacation.
*This idiom is often used with a plan that is unfair to others.
(他人にとって不利になるような計画の話をする時によくこの慣用句を使います。)

**rule out**
to decide something is not possible; to eliminate the idea of.
何かを除外する；あり得ないとする；不可能とする。

ネパール旅行は rule out しないけど、浜辺でリラックスしたいと望んでいた。
I'm not going to rule out a vacation in Nepal, but I was hoping to relax by the beach.

**map out**
to establish a plan of action; to arrange or organize something.
(計画を)立てる、作成する；何かをわかりやすくまとめる、記す。

成功するには、計画を map out して、最後までその計画にそってやり通さないといけない。
You have to map out a plan and stick to it to succeed.

**up in the air**
undecided or uncertain; not yet determined.
未決定で、漠然としている；はっきりしないで不安である；まとまっていない。

ジャニスが田舎へ引っ越す予定は未だに up in the air だ。
Janice's plans to move to the country are still up in the air.
*This idiom is often preceded by the adverb 'still.'
(この慣用句の前には副詞の 'still' がよく来ます。)

**in the works**
being planned or worked on; in progress.
予定されている；進められている。

新しいテクノロジーのおかげで、家庭電化製品を製造している LG社には何か良いことが in the works のようだ。
Looks like something good is in the works for LG Home Appliances with their new technology.

**on the spur of the moment**
impulsively, suddenly; without prior preparation, without prior planning; spontaneously.
出来心で；即座に；突然；衝動的に；準備をせずに。

バリーの広告会社は on the spur of the moment で新しいプロジェクトのために時間を裂くことができる。
Barry's advertising company can make room for new projects on the spur of the moment.

**play it by ear**
to progress gradually depending on the changing circumstances; to improvise; to act as the situation demands.
出たとこ勝負でやる；臨機応変に対応する。

銀行がお金を貸してくれなかったらどうするか分かりません。play it by ear しなければなりません。
I am not sure what to do if the bank does not loan us the money. We'll have to play it by ear.

**wing it**
to do something without preparation; to improvise.
即座で演じる；準備をしていない状態で何かをする；ごまかす。

試験勉強をしなかったので、彼は wing it しなければならなかった。
He didn't study for the exam so he had to wing it.

# Fill in the blanks with the appropriate idioms.

**01** The manager says that my raise is _____ the _____, so let's go celebrate.
部長曰く、僕の昇進が予定されているので、祝いましょうと。

**02** The traveling storyteller is good at _____ _____ wild fantasies and interesting characters for children to imagine as he talks.
語り部は子供たちの想像を膨らませるため、かなり現実離れした幻想的な物語や、おもしろい登場人物を作り上げるのが得意だ。

**03** Making an _____-the-_____ remark can sometimes lead to misunderstandings. Please be careful what you say in the meeting.
とっさの一言が誤解を招くことがあります。会議での発言に気を付けてください。

**04** The lawyers helped me _____ _____ plans for a simple divorce, but it was not simple in the end.
弁護士に、単純な離婚手続きの計画を立てるのを手伝ってもらったにもかかわらず、結局、簡単ではなかった。

**05** Making a clear plan is easy if you map _____ the details.
詳細をまとめておけば、分かりやすいプランを作成するのは簡単だ。

**06** If you always do things _____ _____ _____ of the _____ you'll never finish what you start.
いつも出来心で色々なことをやっていると、始めたことをいつまでも終わらせられないよ。

**07** The police were able to _____ _____ foul play in the death of the three teenagers. The car accident happened because of a recent snowfall.
警察は、若者3人が死んだ事件で不正行為はなかったものと判断できた。交通事故は最近の雪が原因で起こった。

**08** Let's just _____ it by _____ and see what happens after the test results come back.
臨機応変に対応をして、テストの結果が分かってから見てみましょう。

**09** A good cook doesn't need a recipe, they just _____ _____.
料理上手な人はレシピを必要としないで、即座に作ってしまう。

**10** The issue of peace is still _____ in the _____ on the Korean Peninsula.
朝鮮半島では平和意識の問題が未だにあいまいなままだ。

**Answers** 1. in (the) works  2. cooking up  3. off (the) cuff  4. draw up  5. (map) out  6. on the spur (of the) moment  7. rule out  8. play (it by) ear  9. wing it  10. up (in the) air

# Read the following story and refer to the questions below.

### - The Trick is on You

Devon and his friends are always cooking up elaborate* schemes to get out of school or play a joke on someone. Devon is their leader. He has a special ability to draw up a plan on the spur of the moment and can easily convince his friends to help. He usually likes to play it by ear, and yet he never rules out making detailed plans for a practical joke.

Every year on April Fools' Day, he maps out a plan of action to fool the teacher, and this year is no different. The teacher was visibly nervous, as she had heard about his exploits*. It was obvious that he had something in the works, but she couldn't figure out what it was. "Has he come up with some horrible scheme?" she wondered, but she would have to wing it and make her response off the cuff, as she had no idea what was about to happen.

Finally, at the end of the day, the teacher called him over as the children were leaving and asked him to rule out his plans. But in response, he told her that his plan was just to leave her up in the air the whole day and watch her squirm*!

*elaborate 複雑な、入り組んだ   *exploit 偉業、手柄、仕業   *squirm もがく、もじもじする

## Questions about the story

1. What do Devon and his friends like to do?
2. What is Devon good at?
3. Does he usually like to draw up detailed plans?
4. What day is it now? What does Devon usually do on this day?

**5.** What is the teacher worried about? Why?
**6.** What did the teacher wonder? How did she plan to respond?
**7.** What did the teacher do at the end of the day?
**8.** What was Devon's plan? Did it work?

## Questions for discussion

**1.** Have you ever played a practical joke on someone? What was it?
Did you map out a plan or just wing it?
**2.** What types of jokes have been played on you?
How did you respond?
**3.** Do you celebrate April Fools' Day in your country?
Do you have anything in the works this year?
**4.** If someone was looking at you with an evil smirk, what would you do? Why?
**5.** If you could fool anyone in the world, who would you like to fool?
**6.** Do you like to plan out your life/work/vacations or just play it by ear?

### 騙された先生

デボンと彼の友達はいつも学校をサボったり、他人を騙したりするための、複雑な企みを立てていた。デボンが彼らのリーダーだ。即座に計画を立てられる才能を持っていて、いつも協力してもらえるように簡単に友達を説得できた。普通は出たとこ勝負でやるのが好きだけど、いたずらをするためなら詳細な計画を立てることもあった。

毎年、エイプリル・フールになると、先生を騙すための行動を計画していて、今年も例年通りやるつもりだった。先生は彼の仕業のことを聞いていたので、緊張しているのがうかがえた。彼が何かをたくらんでいたのは明らかだったが、それが一体何なのか、彼女には分らなかった。「何か嫌な陰謀を進めているのか？」と彼女は気になったが、何が起こるか予想が付かなかったので、即座に演じてとっさに対応をしないといけなかった。

最終的には、一日の終わりに、子供達が帰途についていると先生は彼を呼び寄せて、計画をやめるように頼んだ。しかしそれに対して、ただ単に何もしないことで、一日中不安になって慌ててもじもじしている先生を見ることが企みだったと彼が言った。

# Chapters 1 - 5

Review Chapters 1-5 and fill in the crossword below.

**Across**

02. Hey kids, want to _____ _____ _____ in Grandpa's old roadster?
03. You don't have to plan everything; sometimes it's fun to do things _____ the _____.
04. Make sure you _____ _____ , even when you drive short distances.
06. What kind of crazy plan have you _____ _____ this time?
09. I'm not ready for the audition. I'll just play it _____ _____.
12. I don't need to look at a recipe! They're chicken wings so I'll _____ _____ .
15. I'm going on a cross-country trip. Will you _____ _____ and give directions?
18. When the Kennedys met for dinner, they _____ _____ half of the restaurant.
19. Mr. Rogers would always _____ _____ into slippers when he got home.
21. The Lone Ranger loved to go off on adventures on the _____ of the _____.
22. When Kane traveled across America, he did it _____ _____ .
23. The whole family would get _____ _____ for church every Sunday morning.

**Down**

01. Ray never remembered to _____ _____ straight, so he got a sore back from slouching.
02. It was so hot working in the garden, I had to _____ _____ my shirt.
03. Fred goes out _____ _____ to meet his wife for lunch on the other side of town.
05. This old motorcycle isn't much to look at, but it's a great way to _____ _____.
07. My first _____ _____ was an old '69 Chevrolet. It was a great car.
08. I need you to _____ me _____ to work. Can you take me?
10. Road _____ is a big problem in congested cities, especially on hot days.
11. If you're going sledding, you'd better _____ _____ because it was quite cold outside.
13. Where did the Green Goblin go? He's _____ _____ Batman's hideout.
14. Will you _____ me _____ at the yoga studio on your way to the mall?
16. _____ _____ so I can sit next to you.
17. My sister _____ great _____ on her way down to Chicago for the weekend.
20. Jill had to _____ _____ 15 pairs of jeans before she could decide which ones to buy.

Making Plans

# 06 Leaving
出発

**get going**
to begin leaving; to begin departing from a place.
(話をやめて)行く；行動を始める；そろそろ行く、どこかを出る。

**get going**しないと、また学校に遅れるよ！
Get going or you are going to end up late for school again!

**be off**
to be departing from the present place or position.
今いるところから離れる、出発をする；「行ってきます」または「お先！」と言う時にI'm off!ということがある。

金曜日の午後、事務所のドアから出て行く時、ジャックは大きな声で「I'm off」と言った。
As Jack walked out of the office door on Friday afternoon, in a loud voice he said, "I'm off."

**take off**
to leave suddenly; to depart in a hurry.
逃げる；急いで去る、出る、出発する。
*Synonym* dash off.

運動場にいじめっ子が現れた時、ティムは**take off**した。
Tim took off when the bully arrived at the playground.

**head out**
to leave a place or area.
出発する；どこかへ出る。

吹雪にも拘らず、エドは**head out**することにした。
Ed decided to head out in spite of the snowstorm.

**head off**
to travel in a particular direction.
どこかへ向かって行く、進む。

サッカーの試合を見るためにトムの家へ**head off**するかもしれないとジェイは夕飯の後に言った。

48　Taking Action

After dinner Jay said that he might head off to Tom's house to watch the football game.
*'Head off' is usually followed by a place or a direction.
(通常'head off'の後に場所または方向が続きます。)

**hit the road**
to leave a place or begin a long road trip or journey.
旅に出る；出発する；出て行く。

ミシェルが話し合いで二人の問題を解決することを断った時、スコットは hit the road した。
When Michelle refused to verbally resolve the issue, Scott hit the road.

**sneak off**
to leave as quietly as possible, without drawing attention to oneself.
こっそり出て行く；こっそり抜ける。

この職員パーティーにはもううんざりだ。9時になったら、誰も見ていない時に sneak off するつもりだ。
I am tired of this staff party. I am going to sneak off at nine o'clock when nobody is looking.

**be long gone**
to have already departed some time ago; to be far away.
とっくに遠くへ離れている；もうすでに出発して遠くへ行っている；大分前に出発している。

まだ彼女のことを愛していると言ってエリカに謝るために、僕は彼女を追って出て行ったが、彼女はすでに be long gone だった。もう彼女は見えなかった。
I ran out after Erica to tell her that I was sorry and that I loved her but she was long gone. I couldn't see her.

Leaving 49

# Fill in the blanks with the appropriate idioms.

**01** Biff and Tina rushed to the train station, but they were too late, the train was already _____ _____.
ビフとティナは電車の駅へ急いだがもうすでに遅すぎた、電車は大分前に出発していた。

**02** If we are going to arrive at the airport on time, we had better _____ the _____ because it's going to be a long trip.
時間通りに空港に着きたいなら、移動に時間が掛かるので、私達はもう出発した方がいいでしょう。

**03** The young couple had hoped to _____ off at the dance, because they wanted to be alone.
若いカップルは二人きりでいたかったので、ダンスパーティーからこっそり抜けたいと思っていた。

**04** As soon as the boys arrived home after school, they _____ _____ to their neighbor's house to play the latest computer game.
男の子達は帰宅したらすぐに、近所の友達の家へ最新のゲームをしに急いで出掛けた。

**05** The students had just finished high school and now they all would head _____ for either work or university.
生徒達は高校を終えたばかりで、今度は全員が就職か大学へ向かって旅立った。

**06** It is getting late; I think that it is time to _____ out of here and go home.
遅くなってきました、もうそろそろここを出て、家に帰る時間だと思います。

**07** If our team is to finish the project on time, we had better _____ _____.
私達のチームが時間通りにプロジェクトを終わらせるならそろそろ行動に出た方がいいでしょう。

**08** As Scott started to leave the office, he raised his hand, waved to all the other employees and announced, "I'm _____."
スコットは事務所を出ようとしていた時に、手を上げて、他の職員に手を振って"お先に!"と言った。

**09** The bank robbers knew that they had only five minutes to _____ off before the police would make it to the crime scene, so they hurried as much as possible.
警察が犯罪現場へ着くまで5分しかないと分かっていたので、銀行強盗は出来るだけ急いだ。

**Answers** 1. (was already) long gone  2. hit (the) road  3. sneak (off)  4. dashed off  5. (head) off
6. head (out)  7. get going  8. (I'm) off  9. take (off)

# Read the following story and refer to the questions below.

### - Being the Boss

After spending all day, and all week long working with the same people, no one wanted to be stuck at the weekend conference. It seemed as though each person had their own important reason why they had to get going.

Being the boss meant that Arthur would have to listen to everyone's excuses regarding why they had to take off. Bill said he needed to hit the road because his babysitter could only work a half day. Marci had to head out early to get to a dentist appointment. Susan dashed off before the speeches even began due to a family emergency. And Beth said that she had made plans before she knew about the conference and was heading off to catch a train for the country.

By lunch, Arthur realized that half of his staff had good excuses for being off. And the other half had snuck off without offering an excuse. They were long gone. He would have to speak to them on Monday morning regarding their professionalism* and commitment* to the company, but for now he'd have to go to the conference himself.

*professionalism プロ意識  *commitment 責任感；義務感

## Questions about the story

1. Why did the employees want to get going?
2. What was Bill's reason for missing the weekend conference?
3. What was Marci's reason for heading out?
4. What did Susan do before the speeches began?
5. Where was Beth going?
6. What did Arthur realize before lunch?

**7.** Why would Arthur have to speak to his employees on Monday?

## Questions for discussion

**1.** Have you ever felt the need to sneak off from an event? Explain.
**2.** What time do you head out for work or school in the morning? What time do you head back home?
**3.** Before you hit the road for a long trip, what are some preparations that you might need to make?
**4.** Where are you headed after this lesson is finished?
**5.** At social events, do you tend to meet most of the people before leaving or do you tend to take off early?

### 上司のする事

1週間の間、一日中同じ人と働いてから、誰も週末の会議に足止めされたくなかった。皆一人ひとり重要な理由があってもう行かないといけないようだった。

皆が急いで行かないといけない理由を、上司であるアーサーは聞かないといけなかった。ビルはベビーシッターが半日しか働けないのでもう出発しないといけないと言った。マルシーは歯医者の予約があったので早く出発しないといけなかった。スーザンはスピーチが始まる前に家族の緊急事態で急いで帰ってしまった。そして、ベスは会議が行われることを知る前から予定を立てていたらしく、田舎へ行く電車に乗るために駅に向かっていた。

お昼の時間までに、アーサーは職員の半数はまともな言い訳があって退社したと言うことに気付いた。もう半数は言い訳もせずに、こっそりと帰ってしまっていた。彼らはもう大分前に退社してしまっていた。月曜日の朝は、プロ意識と、会社に対する責任感について彼らに話をしないといけないが、とりあえずは自分自身が会議に出席しなければならなかった。

# Celebrating Life

**07 生きる喜び**

**live it up**
to have a good time; to spend money freely without worry.
楽しい時を過ごす；贅沢に暮らす；道楽する；豪遊する。

今、会社で昇進し、昇給したところなので、今晩は live it up するつもりだ。
I just got a promotion and pay raise at work, so tonight we are going out to live it up.

**have a ball**
to have a great time.
とても楽しむ。

このナイトクラブで私は have a ball しているわ。また来週もここに踊りに来ましょう。
I'm having a ball at this nightclub. Let's come back here next week to dance.

**have a blast**
to have an excellent time; to have fun.
とても楽しむ。
*Synonym* have a ball.

新しいバイクで、マシューは路上を早く走って have a blast した。
With his new motorcycle, Mathew had a blast riding fast through the streets.

**live life in the fast lane**
to have a very busy social life.
スリルいっぱいの人生を過ごす；遊びほうけて忙しい人生を送る。

有名な映画俳優のように live life in the fast lane 出来たらいいのにと思うけど、私はお金持ちでもありませんし、有名でもありません。
I wish that I could live life in the fast lane like famous movie stars, but I am not rich and I am not famous.

**life of the party**
to be the center of attention at a party.
パーティーの主役である；パーティーを盛り上げる人；皆の注目を集める人。

冗談と明るい性格で皆を笑わせたのでサニーは life of the party だった。
Sunny was the life of the party because her jokes and bright personality made everyone laugh.

**throw a party**
to host a party; to invite guests to an event.
パーティーを企画する；友達などを誘って集まりを主催する。

来週はワンダの誕生日だ、throw a surprise party しよう。
It's Wanda's birthday next week. Let's throw her a surprise party!
*Often words such as birthday, going away, retirement, bachelor and graduation, precede the word party. For example, 'throw a birthday party.'
(多くの場合'party'の前に、誕生日〜、お別れ〜、退職〜、卒業〜、独身最後〜、を付けます。例えば 'throw a birthday party'「誕生日会を開く」と言います。)

**party animal**
someone who enjoys social events such as parties excessively; someone who is the life of the party.
パーティー好きな人；遊びほうけている人。

大学時代、私は本当に party animal だった。週に最低 5 回は飲んでいた。
During my college years I was a real party animal. I drank at least five times a week.

**night on the town**
an evening of social enjoyment in the city; a night of dining and celebrating.
街へ出かけてエンターテインメントを楽しむ夜遊び。

サラリーマン達は night on the town に出掛けていき、さまざまなクラブで楽しい時間を過ごした。
The businessmen were out for a night on the town and enjoyed many different clubs.

**paint the town red**
to have a great time partying or drinking; to wildly celebrate.
お祭り騒ぎする；外出して、たくさん飲んで騒ぐ。

結婚記念を祝いに paint the town red しに出掛けよう。
Let's go out and paint the town red to celebrate our wedding anniversary.

**get out and about**
to leave a building, home etc. for some kind of social activity.
外出する；遊びに出掛ける。

2 週間、毎日書き続けた後、作者は新鮮な空気を吸うために get out and about することに決めた。
After writing all day for two weeks, the author decided to get out and about to breathe some fresh air.

**night owl**
a person who likes to stay up late; a night person.
夜更かしする人；夜型の生活をする人。

夜に電話してくれていいよ、朝の2時か3時まで。私は本当のnight owlだから。
You can call me at night until two or three in the morning. I'm a real night owl.

**early bird**
a person who likes to get up early; a morning person.
朝早く起きる人；朝型の生活をする人。

家族で私だけがearly birdだ。他の皆は夜型のようだ。
I am the only early bird in my family. Everybody else seems to be a night owl.

# Fill in the blanks with the appropriate idioms.

**01** When Phillip graduated, his parents decided to _____ a _____ for him to celebrate.
フィリップが卒業した時、彼の両親は祝いのパーティーを彼のために企画した。

**02** Serena decided that it was time for a night _____ _____ _____ after working hard all week long without any personal time for herself.
一週間の間ずっと自分一人のための時間が全くない状態で一生懸命働いたので、セリーナは夜に出掛けて遊ぶ時がきたと決めた。

**03** Ray used to _____ _____ in the _____ lane before he developed several health problems and ran out of money.
レイは、いくつもの病気を発症した上にお金もなくなってしまった前は、遊びほうけてスリルいっぱいの人生を送っていた。

**04** Everyone thought that Susan was the _____ of _____ _____ when she sang.
スーザンが歌うと皆は彼女がパーティーの主役だと思った。

**05** Jacob went to bed late and often slept in on the weekends because he was such a _____ _____.
ジェイコブはものすごい夜型だったので、よく夜遅くに寝て、週末は遅くまで寝ていた。

**06** After waking up from a six-year coma, Tyler felt he needed to _____ out _____ _____ to see what was going on in the world.
６年間も続いた昏睡状態から目覚めたタイラーは、世界で何が起きているのか知るために外へ出掛けたいと感じた。

**07** My daughter and her boyfriend _____ _____ _____ at their graduation party.
娘とその彼氏は卒業祝いのパーティーをとても楽しんだ。

**08** William wanted to _____ the _____ _____ to impress his date, so he made reservations at a nice restaurant and got a table at the most popular nightclub in town.
ウィリアムは一緒にたくさん騒いで遊んで、デートの相手に良い印象を与えたかったので、素敵なレストランを予約して、町で一番人気のナイトクラブの席を予約した。

**09** When the kids were asked how they enjoyed the amusement park, they said that they _____ a _____.

遊園地がどれぐらい楽しかったか聞かれた子供たちは、とても楽しかったと答えた。

**10** Charles and Marie decided not to go to the party at the fraternity house because they were not _____ _____ and didn't want to socialize with them.
チャールズとメアリーはパーティー好きではなかったし、社交クラブの人達と遊びたくなかったので、社交クラブでのパーティーに行かないことにした。

**11** During the school year, James becomes an _____ _____ because the class he attends begins at eight in the morning.
学校がある間、ジェームズが取っている授業が朝の8時に始まるので彼は朝型になる。

**12** After serving three months in the navy, the sailors had a chance to _____ it _____ for a week during their shore leave in Phuket.
3ヶ月間、海軍で兵役に就いてから、海兵隊員はプーケットでの1週間の上陸休暇の間に楽しく過ごすチャンスがあった。

**Answers**  1. throw (a) party  2. (night) on the town  3. live life (in the) fast (lane)  4. life (of) the party  5. night owl  6. get (out) and about  7. had a ball  8. paint (the) town red  9. had (a) blast  10. party animals  11. early bird  12. live (it) up

# Read the following story and refer to the questions below.

### - Business for Pleasure

Samantha was excited about being her own boss. She had been working with the same company for five years as a public relations consultant, but now she was starting her own company. She still could not believe that someone would pay her to *throw a party* using their money. She was always *the life of the party* and she loved to *live life in the fast lane*, so it made sense that she would do it for a living. Her father had always told her that if she *had a ball* doing something and could make that her career, that she should do it.

Samantha was a *night owl*, and some nights she would go out for *a night on the town* with her clients until 4:00am. Some of her clients just wanted to go out and *paint the town red*, so they hired her to take them around to all of the hottest clubs in the city.

Celebrating Life  **57**

For her business to be successful, Samantha needed her clients to represent themselves as important people with many friends. If her clients seemed to live it up and have plenty of fun, then she was doing a great job, but if her clients had too much to drink and turned into party animals, people would laugh at them and not respect them or her.

The toughest part of her job was when she had to be an early bird after one of her late nights. Some mornings it was difficult for her to get out of bed. Samantha knew that the only way her business would earn a good reputation was if she got out and mingled* with as many influential* people as she could.

*mingle 歓談する；接する  *influential 有力；影響力のある

## Questions about the story

1. Why was Samantha excited about being her own boss?
2. What does she get paid to do?
3. Does she have fun at her job?
4. Why is Samantha good at what she does?
5. What type of person is she?
6. What do her clients like to do?
7. What is the hardest part of her job?
8. How can Samantha earn a good reputation?

## Questions for discussion

1. Are you an early bird or a night owl?
2. Have you ever been the life of a party? Explain.
3. If you were going to paint the town red with a close friend or partner, what would you do?
4. Where is a good place to go to live it up? Have you ever lived it up?
5. When was the last time you threw a party? What kind of party was it?
6. Can an early bird and a night owl ever become a good couple? What might be some problems in such a relationship?

**遊びのような仕事**

サマンサは自営業を始めるのを楽しみにしていた。5年間、同じ会社で広報コンサルタントとして勤めていたが、今、自分の会社を始めようとしていた。誰かのお金を使ってパーティーを企画することでお金がもらえるのは信じられなかった。彼女はいつもパーティーの盛り上げ役だったし、スリルいっぱいの人生が好きだったため、それを職とすることに一理あった。お父さんはいつも自分がやって楽しいことを仕事にできたらやるべきだと言っていた。

サマンサは夜型だったので、客と朝の4時まで遊びに出掛けていた夜も時々あった。客の中には、ただ飲みに行って騒ぎたい人もいたので、彼らは彼女を雇って、町の一番流行っているクラブを彼女に案内してもらっていた。

彼女は、影響力があって、友達もたくさんいるという印象を客に持ってもらわないと、彼女の会社は成功できなかった。客が贅沢な生活をして、人生を楽しんでいるように見えたら、彼女は役を果たしていたが、客が飲みすぎて、遊びほうけてしまうと、笑い者になって、客も彼女も周りの人から尊敬されなくなってしまう。

仕事で一番つらい時は夜更かしした後に早起きしないといけない時だった。なかなかベッドから出るのが大変な朝は何度があった。自分の会社の評判が良くなるには、外へ出掛けて、出来るだけ多くの有力者と接する必要があると分かっていた。

# 08 Health & Fitness

健康とフィットネス

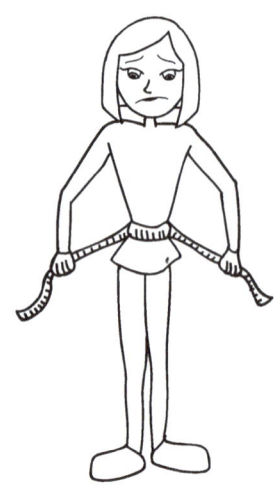

### get in shape
to become fitter or healthier; to improve one's physical condition.
体をきたえる；体調を整える。

マーティンは、テニスの試合に向けて get in shape するのに3週間掛かった。
It took Martin three weeks to get in shape for the tennis match.

### be in shape
to be in a notably good physical condition.
身体的に鍛えられている；(体の)調子がいい。

レスリングの大会で優勝したいのならトムは be in shape でないといけない。
Tom needs to be in shape if he wants to win the wrestling competition.

### out of shape
in a notably poor physical condition; unfit or in poor shape.
運動不足である；身体が鍛えられていない；体調が悪い。

トムは out of shape だったため、レスリングの大会で負けてしまった。
Tom lost the wrestling competition because he was out of shape.

### warm up
to do light exercise or stretching prior to an event or major exercise in order to prepare the body physically.
ウォーミングアップをする；準備体操をする。
*Noun* warm-up.
準備体操；ウォーミングアップ。

ジョギングの前に warm up するためにナンシーはエアロバイクを使う。
Nancy uses a stationary bicycle to warm up before jogging.

60 Taking Action

**workout**
an exercise regime to improve the level of one's fitness.
体力・筋力をつけるためのトレーニング、または練習。
*__Verb__* work out. 筋トレ

タイラーは毎日40分の新しいworkoutメニューを始めた。
Tyler has started a new workout routine that lasts 40 minutes a day.

**put on weight**
to gain weight; to become heavier by gaining fat or muscle.
太る；肥える。

兄がどれほどput on weightしているかを見て私は驚いた。
I was surprised to see how much weight my older brother has put on.

**lay off**
to stop usage and or to avoid contact; to stop doing something.
(不愉快なこと・害になることを)やめる、さける；一休みをする。

ロンは肉ばなれを起こしたので、治るまでしばらくの間、いつもの定期的運動をlay offしないといけない。
Ron pulled a muscle and has to lay off his regular exercise until he heals.
*This idiom may be used for eating certain foods, working specific body parts, general exercise or gym equipment.
(この慣用句は、特定の食べ物、運動法、一般的な運動や筋トレに対して使います。)

**hit the gym**
to go to the gym and exercise earnestly.
ジムに行って真面目に運動・筋トレをする。

しばらく筋トレを怠っていた後、ティムは再び体を鍛えるためにhit the gymすることにした。
After neglecting to work out for some time, Tim decided to hit the gym with hopes of getting back in shape.

**trim down**
to become thinner and weigh less by losing fat.
痩せる；体を引き締める。

セミフォーマルダンスパーティーまでに、ジェシーはtrim downしたいと思っていた。
Jessie wanted to trim down before the semi-formal dance.

**cool down**
to rest for the purpose of lowering one's body temperature, usually after an intense workout or exercise.

ジョンは、バスケをした後、10分掛けてcool downする。
John takes ten minutes to cool down after playing basketball.

(運動後、筋肉をほぐすための軽い)整理運動、クールダウン運動。
***Noun** cool-down.
クールダウン運動。

### out of breath
to be unable to maintain one's normal breathing due to intense exercise.
息が切れる。
*Synonym to be short of breath; lose one's breath.

レースが終わる前に、ビルは out of breath だった。
Bill was out of breath before the end of the race.

### work off
to rid oneself of extra weight or unpleasant feelings by exercising.
(運動をして、脂肪などを)落とす。

ドレスが入るまで、スーザンはウエストを3インチ work off しないといけない。
Susan needs to work three inches off her waist to fit into her dress.

### build up
to gradually increase over time.
徐々に鍛える、増やす、作り上げる。
*Synonym bulk up.

ジェレミーは筋肉を build up するためにウエイト・トレーニングをする。
Jeremy lifts weights to build up his muscles.
*'Build up' generally means to increase muscle mass or overall strength.
(通常'build up'は筋肉量または筋力を増やすと言う時に使います。)

### catch one's breath
to resume normal breathing after physical exertion of some kind.
一息をつく;(激しい運動の後)平常の息に戻る;息を整える。

階段を5階まで上ったジェームズは座って catch his breath の必要があった。
James needed to sit down and catch his breath after climbing five flights of stairs.

### go on a diet
to limit or control the food eaten to improve one's health condition, usually to lose weight.
健康のため、痩せるためにダイエットを始める;食事制限をし始める。
*Synonym be on a diet.
ダイエット中である;食事制限をしている。

ビルは重過ぎたので go on a diet すると決めた。
Bill was too heavy so he decided to go on a diet.

# Fill in the blanks with the appropriate idioms.

**01** Maria was hoping to _____ _____ the extra weight she had gained over the holidays.
マリアは休みの間に増えた体重を落としたいと思っていた。

**02** Lance wanted to be _____ _____ for training camp in the spring.
春の練習合宿に向けてランスは体を鍛えたいと思っていた。

**03** After running two and a half miles, Randy had to stop to _____ his _____ before he could continue or he was going to pass out.
2.5マイル走った後、ランディーはまた走り出す前に、息を整えるために休まないと失神しそうだった。

**04** In North America, June is the most popular month to be on _____ _____.
北アメリカでは6月がダイエットをするのに一番人気の月だ。

**05** Ryan had read a few books about weight training to learn how he could change his workout to _____ _____ his muscle mass.
どういう風にトレーニングを変えたら筋肉の量を増やせることが出来るか知るため、ライアンは何冊か本を読んだ。

**06** Once Earl began to work out with weights hard, he _____ on _____ instead of losing it.
アールは真剣に筋トレを始めてから、痩せる代わりに、体重が増えた。

**07** When Chris' working hours changed, he decided to _____ _____ in the mornings before going to the office.
クリスは勤務時間が変わった時、朝、仕事に行く前に運動をすることに決めた。

**08** A good _____ up is the best way to loosen up you muscles before an intensive workout.
激しい運動の前に筋肉をほぐす一番の方法はしっかりした準備体操だ。

**09** Even though he did not have to go to work on the holiday, Lance decided to _____ the _____ early instead of sleeping late.
休みの日は仕事に行かなくてもよかったが、それでもランスは遅くまで眠るより、朝早くからジムへ行って運動をすることにした。

**10** Nick knew he should _____ down to a smaller size instead of buying new pants.
新しいズボンを買うより、1サイズ痩せた方がいいとニックは分かっていた。

Health & Fitness

**11** Brian's favorite _____-_____ exercise was to walk a few laps around the track with his new MP3 player.

新しいMP3プレイヤーを聞きながら、歩いてトラックを数周するのがブライアンの一番好きなクールダウン法だった。

**12** Marshall knew that once his muscles got sore, he should _____ _____ the heavy weights for a while.

筋肉が痛み始めた時、しばらくの間はきついウエイト・トレーニングを避けた方が良いとマーシャルは知っていた。

**13** After a thirty-minute run on the treadmill, Janet was _____ _____ breath.

ランニングマシーンで30分走った後、ジャネットは息が切れていた。

**14** Since Tom was laid up at home for two months, he has to work out hard to _____ in _____.

トムは2ヶ月間、家で寝込んでいたので、体を鍛えるための筋トレが必要だ。

**Answers** 1. work off  2. (be) in shape  3. catch (his) breath  4. (be on) a diet  5. build up  6. put (on) weight  7. work out  8. warm (up)  9. hit (the) gym  10. trim (down)  11. cool-down  12. lay off  13. (was) out of (breath)  14. get (in) shape

# Read the following story and refer to the questions below.

### - Hitting the Gym

Lance was excited about the fitness gym membership his wife gave him as an anniversary gift. Since his brother had moved away, Lance had not been to the gym to *work out* for a while, so he did not renew his membership and let it expire.

He used to *be in shape* when he and his brother would hit the gym for a *workout* early every morning, so he didn't have to worry about *trimming down* to fit into his clothing. Lance and his wife had tried to stick to a diet, but without the exercise they both ended up *putting on weight*. He decided to take care of the cardiovascular* portion of his *workout* by going for a run soon after he woke up in the morning. He would run the length of his street as a warm up and stretch once he got to the end. The first few times he ran the warm-up distance, he had to stop part way to catch his breath.

Lance was hoping to build up his legs, chest and arms, and to work off the weight he had gained, as well as the inches around his waist. For a cool-down following his workout, Lance usually enjoyed a stroll around the indoor track at the gym. Every third day, Lance would lay off the weights to give his muscles a rest. Now more than ever he was looking forward to their upcoming beach vacation.

*cardiovascular 心臓血管の

## Questions about the story

1. Why has Lance not been to the gym to work out?
2. What didn't he have to worry about before?
3. Why did he and his wife put on weight?
4. What did Lance do for the warm-up portion of his workout?
5. Why did he have to catch his breath?
6. What did he do to cool down after his workout?
7. Why would Lance lay off the weights every third day?

## Questions for discussion

1. Do you work out? What do you do?
2. Do you think that you are in shape or out of shape? Why?
3. How do people put on weight?
4. Do you lose your breath easily? Do you often have to catch your breath?
5. What are some parts of your body that you would like to build up?
6. How long should you lay off weights if you have an injury?
7. How long will it take you to work off your extra weight?

### ジム通い

結婚記念祝いでジム会員登録を妻からもらったことで、ランスはワクワクしていた。弟が引っ越してから、ランスはしばらくの間、ジムへトレーニングをしに行っていなかった。そのため、会員登録を更新しないで期限切れにしていた。
弟と毎日、ジムに通って早朝練習をしていた頃は体が鍛えられていたので、服が着られるように痩せないといけないと、気にしなくってもよかった。ランスと妻は食事制限をしようとしていたが、運動をしていないと、結局2人とも太ってしまった。朝、起きてからすぐにジョギングをすることで、有酸素運動をしようと考えた。自宅の前の道をウォーミングアップとして走って、最後にストレッチをするのだった。初めの数回はウォーミングアップの距離を走っている途中で息を整えるために止まらないといけなかった。
ランスは、脚、胸と腕の筋肉を鍛えて、ウエストに付いた数インチの脂肪も、体重も、落としたいと思っていた。トレーニング後のクールダウンで、普段ジム内のトラックをゆっくり歩くのを楽しんでいた。3日ごとに、彼はウエイトを避けて、筋肉を休ませていた。これで、今度の海への旅行が一層楽しみになった。

# Being Aware 09

気付くこと

**catch someone's eye**
to get someone's attention.
〜誰かに気付かれる；〜と視線が合う；〜の注意を引く；人目を引く。

若い男性は catch her eye しようとして、彼女の前を３度通り過ぎた。
The young man walked by her three times trying to catch her eye.
*Usually with something attractive or pleasing.
(通常、何か魅力的なもののためです。)

**ring a bell**
to sound familiar; to make one remember something.
聞いたことがある；記憶を呼び起こす；はたと思いつかせる；ぴんと来る。

会ったことはないと思うが、彼の名前は ring a bell する。
I don't think I've ever met him, but his name rings a bell.

**dawn on**
to suddenly come to one's mind.
(意味・真実などが)分かり始める；本当のことを気付かせる；(人の心に)急に思い付かせる。
*Synonym cross one's mind.

家族の顔を見るまで、事故の重大さは彼に dawn on しなかった。
The gravity of his accident didn't dawn on him until he saw the faces of his family.

**look out (for)**
to be aware of potential danger; to be ready to notice something.
〜を探す；〜に注意を払う。

北の森で運転している時は、道を横切る鹿に look out for すべきだ。
When driving in the north woods, you should look out for deer crossing the road.
*Most often used as a command.
(通常、命令形で用います。)

### take note (of)
to pay special attention to; to observe carefully.
〜に特別な注意をする；〜にとても気を付ける。

学校の校則と規制を知っておかなければならないのでtake note ofしなさい。
Please take note of the school rules and regulations, as you are expected to know them.

### pay attention (to)
to listen to or observe closely; to concentrate on.
〜に注意する；〜をよく聞く・見る。

先生が言うことにpay attention toして、騒がないようにして下さいよ。
Pay attention to what your teachers say and don't cause trouble.

### stand out
to be readily noticeable; to be easily seen.
目立つ。

赤毛と美貌のおかげで、サンディーは人混みの中でもstand outした。
Sandy's red hair and good looks make her stand out in a crowd of people.
*Often used for things that are quite different from their surroundings and sometimes seen in a negative light.
(周りの環境に順応しないものを指す時によく使います。時々悪い意味でも用います。)

### take in
to absorb into one's mind.
吸収する；取り入れる；〜をじっと見る；〜に聞き入る；理解する。
*Synonym digest (information).

古代神殿の遺跡の中で私は何時間も座り、ただ歴史をtake inしていた。
I sat for hours amid the ruins of the ancient temple grounds, just taking in the history.

### sink in
to become completely understood.
完全に理解される。

アインシュタインの相対性理論の意味がいつまでたってもsink inしない人がいる。
The concept of Einstein's theory of relativity just never sinks in for some people.

# Fill in the blanks with the appropriate idioms.

**01** Give me a minute to let the importance of your words _____ _____ before I respond.

あなたの言葉の重大さを完全に理解してから返事しますから、ちょっと待って下さい。

**02** The new summer fashion is full of bright colors to _____ people's _____.

夏の新しいファッションは、人目を惹きつけるために色鮮やかになっている。

**03** If you don't _____ _____ to the road when you're driving, you'll get into an accident.

運転している時は道路に注意をしないと事故に会いますよ。

**04** When investing legend E.F. Hutton speaks, people _____ _____.

伝説の投資家のE.F.ハットン氏が話すと、人々はとても注意して聴き入る。

**05** The news was so disturbing to hear that it was difficult to _____ _____.

ニュースを聞いていてあまりにも悲惨だったので、理解し難かった。

**06** OK Jimmy, make sure you're not late for the bus and be careful to _____ out _____ cars when you cross the road.

よし、ジミー、バスに遅れないようにね、そして道路を渡る時は車に注意してね。

**07** A combination of high test scores, extra-curricular activities, and community service made his university application _____ _____ from the others.

良い成績と、課外活動と、地域奉仕が全部合わさって、彼の願書は他の大学志望者の願書に比べ、目立った。

**08** Bush? Hmm... Bush; the name _____ _____ _____, but I don't know... wasn't he a singer or something?

ブッシュ？そうだね、ブッシュか、聞いたことあるけど分からないな。歌手か何かじゃなかったか？

**09** The idea for the 'flux capacitor' suddenly _____ _____ him after he fell and hit his head on the toilet.

滑って便座に頭を打った途端に、彼は急に次元転移装置の理論を思い付いた。

**Answers** 1. sink in  2. catch (people's) eyes  3. pay attention (to)  4. take note  5. take in  6. look (out) for  7. stand out  8. rings a bell  9. dawned on

# Read the following story and refer to the questions below.

### - The Mind of a Murderer

In the murder mystery, the main character was Kane, a cop from the seedy* side of town who made it a point* not to stand out. He could blend in with* the crowd and take note of people's habits, looking out for suspicious behavior. He'd come in quietly, take in the scene of the crime, and just see if anything dawned on him. Usually something would catch his eye, but this time there was nothing.

It was only after lots of observation that he'd let his presence be known. Then, he'd try to pay attention to people's reactions. He'd find clues a bit at a time and occasionally something would ring a bell, but so far he still couldn't find the killer.

When the clues started to add up, something became apparent – something that scared him. As the depth of his discovery finally began to sink in, he realized that the mystery had been one within his mind and the characters were hidden within his own personality. He was in fact the murderer, and he would have to pay.

---

*seedy みすぼらしい；汚い；貧弱な；評判の悪い；いかがわしい  *make it a point to do something ～をすることを重視する；必ず～する；きまって～するように努力する  *blend in with ～馴染む；～に溶け込む

## Questions about the story

1. Did the main character stand out in a crowd? Why?
2. What did he use his anonymity to accomplish?
3. What would Kane do at the scene of the crime?
4. Did anything catch his eye?
5. When he let himself be known, what would he pay attention to?
6. What would ring a bell for him?
7. When the clues added up, what crossed his mind?
8. What began to sink in as he realized the identity of the murderer?

## Questions for discussion

1. What would you do to catch the eye of someone you're interested in?
2. What do you take note of when you meet someone new?
3. Do you try to stand out or blend in? Why?
   And how do you do it?
4. When did it dawn on you that Santa Claus wasn't real?
5. As you studied this chapter, did anything ring a bell?

### 殺人犯の心理

殺人推理小説の主人公はケーンだった。彼は町のみすぼらしい地域から来ていて、わざと目立たないように努力をしている警察官だった。人混みに簡単に馴染んで、人々の習慣を観察して、怪しい行動を探すことが出来た。彼は静かに現れて、何かに気付くかもしれないと、犯罪現場を見渡した。いつもなら何か目に入ったか、今回は何もなかった。

徹底的に観察をしてからでないと彼は周りの人に自分がいることを気付かせなかった。そして、彼は人の反応に注意を払った。少しずつ手がかりを見つけて、時々、はたと思い付かせることがあったが、まだ殺人犯が誰かは見つけられなかった。

手がかりが増えると何かが明らかになった - 彼を怖がらせることだった。発見の深層が段々と彼の頭に浸透していき、本当の謎はずっと自分の頭の中にあったのだと気付いた。他の人物も自分自身の性格の中に隠れていたのだ。実は彼が殺人犯だったので、彼が罰を受けなければならなかった。

# 10 Aid & Advice

助けと忠告

### turn to
to consult or ask for help from someone relied upon.
頼る。

もし両親に turn to していなかったら、ダニーはものすごく困っただろう。
Danni would be in big trouble if she didn't have her parents to turn to.

### help someone out
to be helpful or useful; to come to someone's aid.
〜を助ける。
*Synonym lend someone a hand.

その三人の友達はいつも help each other out するようにしていた。
The three friends were always ready to help each other out.
*Usually with a small, simple or easy project.
(通常、単純な、または簡単なことの助けに使います。)

### rally around
to assist somebody in difficulty or in need.
困っている人を助ける、支える；助け・支持を集める；援助のために集まる。

火事のあと、その家族が家を建て直せるように、近所の人は皆 rally around した。
After the fire, the neighbors all rallied around the family to help rebuild their home.

### pitch in
to do one's part; to provide assistance or cooperation.
(金を)出し合う；協力する；仕事に取り掛かる；争いに加わる。
*Synonym chip in.

全員 pitch in すれば、もっと速く家の建築を終えることが出来る。
If everybody pitches in, we can finish building the house much faster.

Taking Action

### take under one's wing
to cultivate someone's ability through teaching; to be watchful for.
〜の世話をする；〜の面倒を見る；〜をかばう；〜を保護する。

昔からの友達が都会へ引っ越した時、私は彼をtake under my wingした。
When my old friend moved to the city, I took him under my wing.

### words of wisdom
intelligent advice from someone's years of experience.
経験がある人からの知識、忠告。

可能な時はいつでも、祖父のところへwords of wisdomをもらいに行った。
Whenever he could, he would go see his grandfather for a few words of wisdom.

### sound someone out
to seek the views and opinions of others; to find out how someone feels about something through careful questioning.
誰かの意見を打診する、さぐる。

どのプレゼントを買うか決める前にsound dad outした方が良いよ。
You'd better sound Dad out before we decide which present to buy.

### speak to
to warn, lecture or provide advice to someone; to consult with someone.
警告をする；(誰かと)相談をする；忠告をする。
*Synonym give (someone) a speaking-to.
説教をする；警告をする。

このヒーターがこわれていることについて家主とspeak toした方が良いです。修理するか、取り替える必要があります。
You'd better speak to the landlord about this faulty heater. It needs to fixed or replaced.
*Usually about something negative.
(通常、何か悪い話をする時に使います。)

### give someone a bum steer
to give false or misleading information or advice; to give poor advice.
お粗末な助言をする；偽りの情報を与える；デマ；間違った助言をする。

私の金融アドバイザーはgive me a bum steerして、私は大金を失った。
My financial advisor gave me a bum steer and I lost a lot of money.

### steer someone straight
to help someone get back on the right track; to provide guidance and direction to someone.
誰かを正しい道へ導く；良い方向へ誰かを案内する。
*Synonym give someone a push in the right direction.

ジョニーは最近、学校をサボっています。steer him straight出来ますか？
Johnny's been skipping school lately. Can you steer him straight?

Aid & Advice

# F ill in the blanks with the appropriate idioms.

**01** Surprisingly, people of lower income _____ _____ the Republican candidate.

意外なことに、収入の低い人が共和党の立候補者を支持した。

**02** Why don't you _____ your boss _____ to see if he's willing to let you take a longer vacation?

もっと長い休みを取らせてくれるかどうか、上司の意見を打診したらどう？

**03** The dying Pope left the masses of people with a few final _____ _____ _____.

瀕死のローマ教皇は最後に民衆に対して知恵の言葉をわずかに残した。

**04** The team project will only get done on time if everyone _____ _____. I'm not going to do it all myself!

チームのプロジェクトは皆が協力しないと時間通りには終わらない。私一人で全部はやらないよ！

**05** Whenever Jessie sees someone with car trouble, he stops to _____ them _____.

車が故障して困っている人を見たらいつも、ジェシーは彼らを助けるために停まる。

**06** When his new student impressed him, Professor Adams _____ _____ under his _____ and taught her everything he knew.

アダムズ教授が新しい生徒から感銘を与えられた時、彼は彼女の面倒を見て、自分の知識を全部彼女に伝えた。

**07** If you don't _____ _____ the boy, I will. I'm sick of his bad attitude and I'm going to give him a long lecture.

あの子に警告をしないのなら、私がするわ。あの態度の悪さにはうんざりだし、彼に長い説教をするわ。

**08** When I got in the accident, I didn't know who I could _____ _____. Thankfully, my girlfriend came to the hospital to take care of me.

事故に会った時、僕は誰に頼ったらいいのか分からなかった。有難いことに彼女が僕の面倒を見るために病院に来てくれた。

**09** Bobby was a born criminal and led a life of robbing and stealing until a tough-talking pastor _____ him _____.

ボビーは産まれつきの罪人で、粘り強く話しをする牧師が正義の道に導いてくれるまでは、物を盗んで生活していた。

**10** After traveling for thirty minutes in the direction that the gas station attendant told him, Tom finally realized that he was given _____ _____ _____.

ガソリンスタンドの店員に言われた方向へ30分走り続けてから、トムは間違った情報をもらったことに気付いた。

Answers  1. rallied around  2. sound (your boss) out  3. words of wisdom  4. pitches in  5. help (them) out  6. took her (under his) wing  7. speak to  8. turn to  9. steered (him) straight  10. (given) a bum steer

# Read the following story and refer to the questions below.

## - The Coffee Shop

Verne and Valerie had been working together at the coffee shop for a year, when they both decided to quit and open their own brew house. Their friends all rallied around them to lend a hand with the opening. At the opening party, they recalled how they had met.

The first day they had worked together was a bit of a fiasco*. Valerie spent half the day trying to steer Verne straight as he made mistake after mistake, while the other workers pitched in where they could. At the end of the day, the manager gave him a speaking-to. Verne was so nervous about losing his job that he turned to Valerie for help. She took him under her wing and soon her encouraging words of wisdom paid off.

Eventually, he became the top employee and an expert barista*. He learned all there is to know about coffee and became an advisor for the other employees as well as his boss. He became popular with the customers for always being willing to help out with little tidbits* of information. So when Valerie tried to sound him out on the idea of a shop, he was more than ready to help. After all he was always known as someone who would never give anyone a bum steer!

*fiasco 失敗；不面目な結末；大混乱  *barista コーヒーを入れる人  *tidbit 断片；さわり；一口のうまい食べ物

## Questions about the story

1. What did Verne and Valerie's friends do at the opening of their shop?
2. Was Verne's first day a success?
3. What did Valerie and the other employees do to help out?
4. After Verne got the speaking-to from the manager, what did he do?
5. What did Valerie do for him? How did she do it?
6. How did he become popular with the customers?
7. When Valerie came to him to sound him out, what was his response?

## Questions for discussion

1. Has anyone ever taken you under his or her wing? Would you ever take someone under yours?
2. Who do you go to to sound out your problems?
3. Do people in your country pitch in to help a neighbor in need?
4. What would you do if your best friend got in trouble with the law and turned to you to hide from the police? Why?
5. Have you tried to steer someone straight? Why? What was the outcome?
6. Have you ever purposely given someone a bum steer?

### コーヒーショップ

一年間一緒にコーヒーショップで働いた時、バーンとバレリーは二人で辞めて、一緒にコーヒーショップを開くことにした。彼らの友達は皆、彼らを支えるために集まって、オープニングを手伝った。オープニング祭で彼らは自分たちの出会いについて振り返った。

初めて一緒に働いた日はちょっとした大混乱だった。バレリーは半日掛けて、他の店員とも助け合いながら、失敗を繰り返すバーンを正そうとしていた。その日の終わりに彼は店長に説教をされた。バーンは首になるのがあまりにも不安だったので、助けてもらおうとバレリーに頼った。彼女は彼の面倒を見て、そのうち彼女の励ましと知識の言葉が功を奏した。

最終的に彼は一番優秀な店員になって、コーヒーの名人になった。コーヒーについての知識を出来るだけ増やして、他の店員たちや、店長の相談役になった。いつもちょっとした豆知識を提供することで、客からの人気を集めた。だから店を開くことに関してバレリーが彼の様子を探った時、彼はとても協力的だった。結局、彼は決してお粗末な助言をするような人ではないと人々に常に知られていた！

# Chapters 6 - 10

Review Chapters 6-10 and fill in the crossword below.

## Across

01. I just got a bonus! Let's go _____ the town _____.
05. _____ _____ _____ Jack, and don't come back no more.
06. The children _____ _____ behind the shed to smoke.
08. OK kids, make sure you _____ _____ for cars when you cross the road.
10. Bears _____ _____ weight in the fall so they can hibernate all winter.
11. I've got to _____ _____ the extra weight I gained during the holidays.
13. Honey, you don't need to go _____ _____ _____. Just work out and you can eat all you want.
15. Let's _____ the boss _____ before we decide on a course of action.
18. We'd better _____ _____ of here before it gets too dark to see in these woods.
19. When I saw men in trench coats come into the bank, I _____ _____.
20. It suddenly _____ _____ Louis that the blue mold in the petri dish might be useful.
21. We had better _____ _____ if we're going to make it to the airport on time.
22. I owe my success to a teacher who helped to _____ me _____.
23. I like to walk around a city to _____ _____ the architecture.
24. The Czech people _____ _____ communism for its Utopian ideals.

## Down

01. Dave got a phone call and suddenly _____ _____.
03. I just finished my dissertation, so tonight I'm going to _____ it _____.
04. After running from the bear, I couldn't _____ my breath for a few minutes.
07. We should _____ _____ _____ for John since he's leaving for Europe next week.
09. When I got arrested, I didn't know who to _____ _____, so I called you.
12. James Dean wanted to live life in the _____ _____, but that's how he died.
13. Sitting at home won't help you get over her; you've got to get _____ _____ _____.
14. If everyone _____ _____, we'll get the project done in no time.
16. This year, I'm going to _____ _____ _____ so I can fit into my old jeans.
17. Paris who? Paris Hilton. Hmm... the name _____ _____ _____, but I don't know her.

# 11 Looking For & Finding

探すこと、見つけること

**go over**
to review; to examine; to study.
見直す；復習する。

アンダーソン先生は、間違いがないかどうか確かめるため、提出する前に解答用紙をもう一度 go over するように生徒に注意した。
Mr. Anderson warned his students to go over their test papers one more time to check for mistakes before handing them in.

**look up**
to search for and find information.
調べる；情報を検索する。

スティーブンは昔の全同級生の住所をインターネットで look up して、クリスマスカードを送ることにした。
Steven decided to look up the addresses of all his old classmates on the Internet and send them a Christmas card.
*This idiom is widely used to search reference books or information on the Internet.
(この慣用句は参考図書やインターネットを使って情報を探す時によく使われます。)

**look into**
to probe; to investigate.
調査する；検討する；調べる。

財務委員の会員による資金の不正管理の供述ついて、市の役員が look into している。
City officials are looking into to the allegations of money mismanagement by members of the financial committee.

78　Taking Action

### be after
to be looking for; to be in pursuit of.
探す；追う。

銀行強盗の容疑者として20代後半の白人男性2人を be after だと警察はマスコミに言った。
Police told the media that they are after two white males in their late twenties as suspects in the bank robbery.

### find out
to learn from knowledge obtained from investigating or searching.
(調べたり、検索したりして得た)情報や資料を使って知識を増やす；探り出す。

次の休みにアジアの国を訪ねようと思っているのなら、インターネットを使えば必要な情報は何でも find out できるよ。
If you plan to visit a country in Asia on your next vacation, you can find out all of the information that you need by using the Internet.

### come up with
to discover; to invent; to learn.
思いつく；見つける；発明する；提案する；出くわす。
*Synonym think up.

職員が会議で思いつくままに意見を出し合う時はいつも、タミーは一番良い提案を come up with します。
Tammy always comes up with the best ideas whenever our staff has a brainstorming meeting.

### turn up
to appear or to be found after previously being misplaced or lost.
(失くしていたものが)見つかる；出てくる；現れる。

失くした財布は5年後、家のソファのクッションの下に挟まって turn up した。
My lost wallet turned up five years later, lodged beneath the family sofa cushion.

### run across
to discover by chance or unexpectedly.
予想しない時に見つける；偶然見つける；偶然会う。
*Synonym come across.

タンスを整理して片付けている時に、ジェフは家族の古い写真を run across した。
Jeff ran across some old family photos while he was cleaning out the closet.

### come by
to acquire; to get.
手に入れる；入手する；得る。

その新しい携帯はどのようにして come by したの？確かその機種はまだ発売されていないはずだと思ったが。
How did you come by that new mobile phone? I thought that model was not on sale yet.

Looking For & Finding

**read up on**

to obtain information about a certain topic in detail through reading.
(読書をして)何かについて勉強をする、知識を得る。

恥ずかしい間違いをしないように、ベトナムへ発つ前に、ニックは地元の文化と習慣について read up on するつもりだ。

Before Nick travels to Vietnam, he will read up on the local culture and customs so that he doesn't make any embarrassing mistakes.

# Fill in the blanks with the appropriate idioms.

**01** If my parents _____ _____ that I got another speeding ticket, they will kill me!
もしまたスピード違反切符を切られたことを親に知られたら私は殺される！

**02** Chris was eager to check if the comic book convention had the comic book that he _____ _____.
クリスは、捜し求めていた漫画が漫画本大会にあるかどうか、ものすごく確かめたいと思っていた。

**03** Police have discovered a hole in the nudist colony wall. Local investigators are _____ _____ it.
警察は裸体主義者村の壁に穴が開いているのを発見した。地元の捜査官がそこを調査している。

**04** Alice _____ by a fancy antique table at the local flea market last Saturday.
先週の土曜日のフリーマーケットでアリスは手のこんだ年代物のテーブルを手に入れた。

**05** Don't worry if you can't find Tim; I'm sure that he will _____ up at some point when the party dies down.
ティムを見つけられなくても気にしないで。パーティーが静まってから、いつか現れるに違いない。

**06** Marcy ran _____ an old friend while she was shopping at the mall with her mother.
母とショッピングセンターで買い物をしている時、マーシーは昔の友達に偶然会った。

**07** Philip _____ up _____ a good title for the newspaper article that he was writing.
フィリップは、書いていた新聞の記事にぴったりの題名を思いついた。

**08** Sam said that he needs to _____ _____ some of the math formulas that we learned in class to prepare for the test.
テスト準備のために、授業で習った数学の公式を復習する必要があるとサムは言った。

**09** Anthony made sure to _____ up _____ as much information about the stock market as he could before he decided to invest.
投資する前に、アントニーは株取引市場について出来るだけの情報を読んで勉強するようにした。

**10** Sal _____ _____ the words that he didn't know in the dictionary.
サルは、分からなかった単語を辞書で引いて調べた。

**Answers** 1. find out  2. was after  3. looking into  4. came (by)  5. turn (up)  6. (ran) across
7. came (up) with  8. go over  9. read (up) on  10. looked up

# Read the following story and refer to the questions below.

### - Inside information

Everyone at the office seemed to be on edge. With two top managers leaving, there was room for almost anyone to get a promotion. Douglas ran across a memo containing the details of the promotions* that had been placed in his mailbox by mistake.

First, Douglas searched through the most recent emails to try and read up on any warning signs that may have been there about the promotions. Then he decided to have his friend go over the memo to see what he thought about it. After looking up as much background information as they could find, both men decided that it was in their best interest* to make sure no one else found out about the memo and plan for promotions. This would only increase their chances of being promoted themselves.

It wasn't long before the site supervisor realized that she had made a mistake with the placement of the memo. That realization caused her to stop by and speak with each employee personally in order to come by more information. By the afternoon, Douglas noticed her poking around* in the room where the mailboxes were. The supervisor came up with an excuse for the missing memo that satisfied the manager, but she was after the person who took the original memo. She hoped that the missing memo would turn up because she was spending the rest of the day looking into the situation.

---

*on edge 緊張している；ぴりぴりしている  *in one's best interest ～にとって一番得である；～のことを一番考えた  *poke around 探る

## Questions about the story

1. How did Douglas know about the details of the promotions?
2. Once Douglas obtained the new information, what did he do first?
3. What did his friend do with the memo?
4. What did both men decide was in their best interest?
5. Describe the actions of the site manager.
6. What was the site manager hoping for?
7. How was the site manager going to spend the rest of her day?

## Questions for discussion

1. Have you ever run across something that you were not supposed to see?
2. Describe what you would do to find out more information on a topic.
3. Describe a situation where someone would come up with an excuse for something that was missing.
4. Have you ever waited for something that was missing to just turn up?
5. Describe a situation where you found out something that surprised you. How did you find out or come by this information?
6. Describe several methods to obtain information about a company that is listed on the stock market.
7. Before going on vacation to another country, what are some ways to find out about your travel destination?

### 内部情報

社員全員が緊張しているようだった。役員が2人もいなくなることで、ほとんど誰もが昇進できるポストがあった。ダグラスは、昇進の情報が載った社内メモが誤って自分の郵便受けに投函されていたのを偶然見つけた。

まず、ダグラスは最近のメールを探って、昇進があるかもしれないことを暗示するような情報がないか読み取ろうとした。その後に友達にもメモを見てもらって、彼がどう思うか聞くことにした。背景情報を出来るだけ調べてから、他の誰にもメモのことや、昇進が予定されていることを知られないようにするのが、2人にとって一番得策だと考えた。自分達が昇進するという可能性のみを増やすのだった。

まもなく、係長はメモを配布した時の自分の過ちに気付いた。これに気付いた彼女は、社員一人ひとりのところへ立ち寄って、個人的に話をして情報を入手した。午後には、彼女が郵便受けのある部屋を探している様子にダグラスは気付いた。なぜメモがなくなったかを部長に納得させる言い訳を考えついたが、彼女はメモの原文を持っている人を探していた。その日の残りの時間を費やして捜索していたので、行方不明のメモが現れるよう、彼女は願っていた。

# 12 Making an Effort

努力すること

**get around to**
to find time for something, especially after a delay; to do at last or slowly begin to get done.
〜をする余裕・時間を見つける；〜に手が回る；〜するに至る。

時間がある時に芝生を刈ることに get around to するよ。私を煩わすのを止めて。
I will get around to cutting the grass when I have time. Please stop bothering me.

**take the bull by the horns**
to take charge of a situation and confront a problem head-on; to face a difficulty and grapple with it without avoiding it.
勇敢に難局にあたる；問題に真正面に立ち向かう；問題を避けずに立ち向かう。

何年間も体重が重いことで悩んだ末、コリンは take the bull by the horns して痩せようと決めた。
After having a problem with his weight for several years, Collin finally decided to take the bull by the horns and lose the extra weight.

**burn the midnight oil**
to work late into the night.
夜遅くまで仕事・仕事をする。

仕事の期限に間に合うようにエリックと同僚は burn the midnight oil しなければならなかった。
Eric and his co-workers had to burn the midnight oil to meet the deadline at work.

### burn the candle at both ends
to do two or more full-time jobs, usually working day and night; to exhaust one's energies or resources by leading a hectic, busy life.
朝早くから夜遅くまで働く；精力を使い果たす；無理をする。

学校に通いながら常勤の仕事をしようとして、ジェイは本当にburn the candle at both endsしている。
Jay is really burning the candle at both ends, trying to work a full-time job and attend school at the same time.

### go all out
to give one's best effort.
やっきになる；全力を尽くす；最大の力を発揮する。
*Synonym all-out (adj.)

試合の後半でタンのサッカーチームはgo all outすることにした。
Tan's soccer team decided to go all out during the second half of their game.

### keep (it) up
to maintain in good condition; to continue doing a good job.
維持する；続ける；調子よく続ける；頑張り続ける。

報告書に目を通してから、ドンの上司は笑顔で「いい仕事をkeep upしろよ。」と言った。
Don's boss smiled after looking over the report and said, "Keep up the good work."

### halfhearted
feeling or showing little interest or enthusiasm; lackadaisical and unenthused.
熱が入らない；気乗りのしない；やる気のない。

アトキンズさんはhalfheartedなやり方で仕事での問題解決に取り組んだ。
Mr. Atkins took a halfhearted approach to solving the problem at work.

### not lift a finger
to make no efforts to work or assist someone.
少しも労をとらない；～をしようとしない；全く手を貸さない。

アレックスが家事の手伝をnot lift a fingerした。とジュディーは言い張る。
Judy claims that Alex doesn't lift a finger to help with the housework.

### drag one's feet
to procrastinate; to act or work with intentional slowness; to deliberately hold back or delay due to a lack of desire to work.
足を引きずる；わざとぐずぐずする；頑張らない；やる気がない。
*Synonym drag one's heels; drag one's ass. (slang)

ティモシーはいつも朝、会社でdrag his feetしているように見える。
Timothy always seems to drag his feet at work in the morning.

# F ill in the blanks with the appropriate idioms.

**01** The office workers made a _____ effort when they were forced to work late on Christmas Eve.
イブの夜に遅くまで残業をさせられたサラリーマンは仕事にやる気がなかった。

**02** Tom said that he would eventually _____ _____ to cleaning his room if he had time.
時間がある時にいつか部屋の掃除にまで手が回るよとトムは言った。

**03** Alex's three sons _____ all _____ to prepare the best birthday celebration that they could for their father.
アレックスの3人の息子は、父親に最高の誕生日祝いをするために全力を尽くした。

**04** I should take _____ _____ _____ the horns and finish doing all of my homework before Sunday.
私は宿題に真正面から取り掛かって日曜日までに終えるべきだ。

**05** Brad likes to be lazy on the weekend. He won't _____ _____ _____ to do any of the chores around the house.
週末ブラッドは怠けるのが好きだ。家の中の家事に全く手を貸さない。

**06** Patricia's parents scolded her for continuing to _____ her _____ at school. Her grades were slipping and she needed to study more.
ずっと今までパトリシアが学校で頑張っていないので、両親は叱った。成績が落ちていたので、彼女はもっと勉強をする必要があった。

**07** Since Jake had only been working for two weeks, it was quite hard for him to _____ _____ with the other workers.
まだ働き始めて2週間しか経っていなかったので、ジェークにとって、他の従業員と同じ調子で仕事をするのはかなり難しかった。

**08** After _____ the _____ _____ _____ ends for several months trying to save money to buy his girlfriend Angela a diamond engagement ring, Chris nearly broke down with exhaustion.
彼女のアンジェラのためにダイヤの婚約指輪を買おうと、何ヶ月間も朝から夜まで働いてクリスは過労で倒れそうになった。

**09** Sam was _____ _____ _____ oil, trying to finish his proposal on time to submit to his boss.
上司に提出するための提案書を終えようとサムは夜遅くまで働いていた。

**Answers** 1. halfhearted  2. get around (to)  3. went (all) out  4. (take) the bull by (the horns)  5. (won't) lift a finger  6. drag (her) feet  7. keep up  8. burning (the) candle at both (ends)  9. burning the midnight (oil)

# Read the following story and refer to the questions below.

### - Back to School

Ever since Min and Andrew decided to go back to school part time, it was tough for them to keep up the payments on their large house. They always knew they wanted to complete their schooling, but never got around to applying. Whenever one of them had been ready to go back to school, the other only felt halfhearted about making the change.

This time, it had been Min who was dragging her feet about making the decision. Andrew decided to take the bull by the horns and convince Min that in the end, they would both be happier and would secure better jobs with their education. Andrew went all out and prepared spreadsheets of potential earnings and investments that they could make once their schooling was complete. He also had to promise to help out around the house because until then he had not lifted a finger to help with housework.

They knew that burning the candle at both ends was not the answer to doing well in school, so they decided to try and sell their house and reduce their large payments. Min and Andrew knew they would only have to burn the midnight oil at the factory for a few more months and that made them happy.

## Questions about the story

**1.** What had delayed Min and Andrew's decision until now?
**2.** What was tough for them to continue doing?
**3.** Which one was dragging their feet about the decision?

Making an Effort

**4.** What did Andrew do to convince Min?
**5.** What special promise did Andrew make to Min?
**6.** What kind of jobs were Min and Andrew planning to leave? And what made them happy?

## Questions for discussion

**1.** Did you get (or are you getting) the education you wanted?
**2.** If you could go back and choose another field of study, what would it be?
**3.** Do you ever burn the midnight oil at your current job (or at school)?
**4.** Have you ever taken the bull by the horns to do something difficult?
**5.** Have you ever gone all out to accomplish a lofty goal? What was it?
**6.** What are some small jobs that you need to do, but have not gotten around to doing yet?
**7.** What would be worth burning the candle at both ends?
**8.** What do you feel halfhearted about?

---

復学

ミンとアンドリューが学校へ復学すると決めてから、大きな家のローンの返済が難しくなっていた。学校教育を終えたいと思っていたものの、なかなか入学書類を出すまでに至らなかったのだ。一人が復学する準備が出来ていると感じた時、もう一人は生活の変化に乗り気になれなかった。

今回の決断はミンがくずくずしていたのだ。アンドリューは真正面から問題と立ち向かって、教育を終えた方が二人は幸せになれるし、良い仕事に就けるとミンを説得しようと決めた。アンドリューはやっきになって、学校教育を終えれば可能になる将来の見込み収入と投資支出の表計算を用意した。さらに、今まで家事を全然やらなかったので、彼は家事を手伝うと約束をしなければいけなかった。

無理をすれば学校の勉強もうまく行かないと彼らは分かっていたので、家を売って、支払額を下げようと考えた。工場で夜遅くまで働く生活も後、数ヶ月しか必要ないと知って、ミンとアンドリューは幸せだった。

# Making Mistakes 13 間違えをする

**do something over**
to do again; to redo to correct a mistake.
やり直す。

関係はうまく行かなかったが、もしもdo it over出来るなら、そうしたかった。
The relationship failed, but if I could do it over, I would.

**screw up**
to make a mess of something or foul up through incompetence or carelessness.
〜に失敗をする；〜を台無しにしてしまう。

ケリーはアメリカにいる友達に電話をする時間をscrew upして彼女を起こしてしまった。
Kerry screwed up the time, calling her friend in the US and waking her up.

**goof up**
to make a mistake or blunder; to act foolishly.
へまをする；どじを踏む；馬鹿げたことをする。
*Noun* goof-up.
不注意な失敗；どじ；へま。

ジョンはまた学校でgoof upした。試験勉強をするのを忘れ、不合格だった。
John goofed up at school again. He forgot to study for the test and failed it.

**be on the wrong track**
to be doing something in a way that will eventually lead to failure; to be going the wrong way or following the wrong set of assumptions.
間違った方向に向いている；間違ったやり方をしている；間違った思い込みをしている。

クルーゾー警部はいつもbe on the wrong trackのように見えても、泥棒をうまく捕まえることができる探偵だ。
Inspector Clouseau is a detective who always seems to be on the wrong track, but still manages to capture the thief.

### make a mess of
to confuse or bungle; to mess up.
～台無しにする；～し損なう；混乱して～をめちゃくちゃにする。

ジャニスはお酒と麻薬に溺れてしまって、人生をmake a mess ofした。
Janice made a mess of her life when she got into drugs and alcohol.

### mix up
to confuse or bewilder; to exchange one thing for another by mistake.
～を混乱させる；～をごちゃ混ぜにする；～を間違える。
*Noun mix-up.
誤解；誤り；(順序の)間違い。

可愛い女の子が私に微笑むと、私は言葉をmix upして話せない。
When a pretty girl smiles at me, I mix up my words and can't speak.

### put one's foot in one's mouth
to say something foolish or wrong; to make an embarrassing verbal blunder.
不謹慎なことを言う；しくじる；へまなことを言う。

人の前で話さないといけない時、私はいつもput my foot in my mouthしてしまう。
Every time I have to talk in public, I put my foot in my mouth.

### mess up
to make a mess of; to bungle or do something incorrectly.
混乱する；ごたごたする；へまをする。
*Noun mess-up.
混乱状態；ごたごた；へま。

ケリーがスケジュールをmess upしたので、今、全員が混乱して遅れている。
Kelly messed up the schedule, and now everyone's confused and late.

### faux pas
an embarrassing error that is not socially correct.
(社交上の)失言、非礼。

大使館の晩餐会で大佐は小さなfaux pasをしてしまった。
The Colonel made a small faux pas at an embassy dinner.
*This idiom comes from French, but is in common usage in English (pronounced "fo-pa").
この慣用句はフランス語から来ていますが、英語でもよく使われて「フォーパ」と発音します。

### slip of the tongue
an accidental blunder in speech; an unintended comment.
間違えて言ったこと；うっかり口を滑らして言ったこと。

リズが「おかしく」見えるとジャックは言った。本当は「かしこく」見えると言いたかった。ただのslip of the tongueだった。
Jack said that Liz looked 'silly.' He meant to say she looked 'savvy'. It was just a slip of the tongue.

**get one's wires crossed**
to have a misunderstanding; to become mistaken and confused about something through a misunderstanding.
混乱して誤解する；言い間違いを生じる。

ジェシカを理解できない。私達はいつも **get our wires crossed** している。
I don't understand Jessica. We just keep getting our wires crossed.

**bark up the wrong tree**
to be wasting time and effort by pursuing the wrong person or thing.
見当違いなことをする；間違ったこと・物・人を求めて時間を無駄にする；おかど違いの非難をする。

スパーキー、私が代わりにあなたの宿題をしてあげると思っているのなら、君は **bark up the wrong tree** しているよ。
Sparky, you're barking up the wrong tree if you think I'm going to do your homework for you.

**not think straight**
not think clearly.
理路整然と考えられない；ちゃんと考えることが出来ない。

部屋の中がうるさくて混雑している時、私は **not think straight** する.
I can't think straight when there is noise and confusion in the room.

Making Mistakes

# Fill in the blanks with the appropriate idioms.

**01** Watch your words, men; any social slip or _____ _____ could ruin our mission.

いいか、お前ら、言葉遣いに気を付けろよ。どんな失言でも社交の非礼でも、俺達の使命は台無しになるから。

**02** Mom would always yell at Greg and his brother for eating the neighbor's apples, but she was _____ up the _____ _____, as it was Dad eating them, not the kids.

お母さんはいつもグレッグと弟にお隣さんのりんごを食べないように怒鳴っていたが、食べていたのは子供達ではなくお父さんだったので、おかど違いの非難をしていた。

**03** If you continue to _____ _____ on the project, you'll be removed from the group.

そのプロジェクトでどじを踏み続ければ、グループから外しますよ。

**04** A simple _____-_____ left Sunny sitting in a jail cell while the real criminal was still free.

単純な誤解のせいで、本当の犯人が自由でいながら、サニーが刑務所の独房に入れられていた。

**05** I messed _____ my calculations so often that I couldn't keep money in my bank account.

私はあまりにも頻繁に計算間違いをしたため、銀行口座にお金を残しておくことが出来なかった。

**06** Sherry _____ up on her math test.

シェリーは数学のテストを台無しにしてしまった。

**07** Freddy _____ _____ _____ of things when he tried to date more than one girl.

一人以上の女の子と交際をしようとした時、フレディーはめちゃくちゃなことをしてしまった。

**08** When dealing with international business, it's very easy for people of different cultures to _____ _____ wires _____.

国際ビジネスをする上で、違う文化の人々の間で誤解が生じるのはよくある事だ。

**09** If you make a mistake you'll have to _____ it _____ again.

間違いをすれば、やり直さなければならない。

**10** Ross really _____ _____ foot _____ _____ _____ when he called his fiancée by the wrong name.

婚約者を違う名前で呼んだ時、ロスは本当にしくじってしまった。

**11** A simple slip _____ _____ _____, like saying 'sex' when you mean 'six', can create a big problem.

「シックス」と言いたいのに「セックス」と言ってしまうように、単なる言い間違いでも大きな問題を招くことがある。

**12** If your reasoning is poor, you will often be on _____ _____ _____ when you are looking for answers to questions that you may have.

推理が下手ならば、質問の答えを探している時には間違った思い込みをしていることが多い。

**13** Without proper training, a fireman will _____ be able to _____ _____ in a fire.

ちゃんとした訓練を受けていなければ、消防士は火災中に理路整然と考えることが出来ない。

**Answers** 1. faux pas  2. barking (up the) wrong tree  3. goof up  4. mix-up  5. (messed) up  6. screwed (up)  7. made a mess (of)  8. get their (wires) crossed  9. do (it) over  10. put his (foot) in his mouth  11. (slip) of the tongue  12. (be on) the wrong track  13. not (be able to) think straight

# Read the following story and refer to the questions below.

### - Leave it to Freud

The famous psychiatrist,* Dr. Sigmund Freud, said that all slips of the tongue are psychological expressions of our real desires, yet others insist that they are simple cases of mixed-up speech. A faux pas, which results in your foot in your mouth could very easily be a demonstration of some hidden desire, but it could also be a simple screw-up. People often don't think straight when they are in stressful positions and goof up when trying to speak.

If Freud is right, the result would be the same even if they had a chance to do it over. I think he was on the wrong track, as people will often get their wires crossed with others. I know I mess up all the time too, and yet my mistakes are just that – mistakes. Maybe he wants a reason for everything, but he just made a mess of it in the process. However, if you think I have the answer, you're barking up the wrong tree!

*psychiatrist 心理学者；精神科医

## Questions about the story

1. What does Freud think slips of the tongue really are?
2. What do others believe they are?
3. What can a faux pas result in?
4. What happens when people are in stressful positions?
5. What does the writer think about Freud?
6. How is Freud on the wrong track?
7. Does the writer have the answer to the problem? What does he say?

## Questions for discussion

1. Have you ever made a slip of the tongue? Give an example.
2. What kind of mess-ups have you seen or heard people make?
3. Which idea do you think is correct in the story?
4. Is it true that when you're drunk you're more likely to speak the truth? Why? Can you think straight when you're drunk?
5. What is the biggest or funniest goof-up you've ever made?

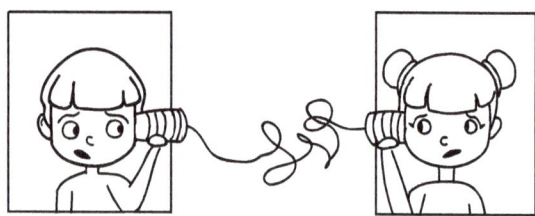

**フロイドにお任せ**

有名な心理学者のシグムンド・フロイド博士によると、全ての言い間違いは心理的な本能の欲望の表現である。しかしそれに対して他の人はただ単に言葉を間違えているのだと言う。失言をして不謹慎なことを言ってしまうのは隠れていた欲望の証だと簡単に言えもするが、同時に単なる間違いかもしれない。ストレスがある状況にいると多くの人は理路整然と考えることが出来ず、話そうとするととじを踏むのだ。

フロイドが正しければ、もし言い直せたとしても同じ結果になるはずだ。人々はよく混乱して言い間違えるので、フロイドは間違った思い込みをしていたと思う。私自身もよくへまをすることがあるのは分かっているが、私の間違いは、その通り、単なる間違いなのだ。彼はどんなことでも論理付けしようとしているうちに混乱したのかもしれない。しかし私から答え求めているのなら時間の無駄だよ。

# Risk & Reward

**14 リスクと報酬**

**be iffy**
to be uncertain or undecided; to not be totally good, truthful or suitable.
不確かである；あやふやしている；疑わしい；不真面目な；適していない。

「あなた、子供達は宿題したと思う？」
「わからない…ちょっとbe iffyだ。」
"Honey, do you think the kids did their homework?"
"I don't know… it's kind of iffy."

**fifty-fifty**
equal in chances of both success and failure.
五分五分の；半々の；五分五分の見込み。

夏に北アフリカへ行けば、マラリアに罹るかどうかはfifty-fiftyだ。
If you go to North Africa in the summer, it's fifty-fifty that you'll get malaria.

**miss out (on)**
to fail to take advantage of a good opportunity.
～を見逃す；～を逸する。

よお、ダン、君は学校での騒動をmiss out onしてしまったみたいだね。大喧嘩があったよ。
Hey Dan, you missed out on all the excitement at school. There was a big fight!

**chances are (that)**
to be likely to be true.
見込みである；可能性がある；可能性が高い。

アラスカではホワイトクリスマスになるchances areだ。
Chances are that there will be a white Christmas in Alaska.
*If 'that' is not used, a comma follows 'are'.
('That'を使わない場合、'are'の後にコンマが続きます。)

### stand a chance
to be possible; to have a chance to win, survive or achieve.
〜の可能性が十分にある；勝つ見込みがある；成功する見込みがる；生き延びる可能性がある。

フレッドは宝くじが当たる stand a chance しないけど、それでも毎週金曜日に宝くじ券を買う。
Fred doesn't stand a chance of winning the lottery, but he buys a ticket every Friday anyway.

### put all one's eggs in one basket
to risk everything on one single venture.
全てを一回に賭ける；リスクを分散しない。

マクミラングループの経理部長は put all their eggs in one basket して、全てを失ってしまった。
The Macmillan Group's finance manager put all their eggs in one basket and lost everything.

### pipe dream
a dream that is impossible to achieve; a vain hope.
非現実的な計画；夢物語；夢想；世迷い言。

ロックスターになると言うダンの pipe dream は現実になることはなかった。
Dan's pipe dream to be a rock star never came true.

### irons in the fire
several maturing projects at once.
一度にいくつかの仕事や計画(に手を出して)；いくつかの可能性(を確保して)。
*Synonym balls in the air; juggling many things at once.

神経衰弱になるまで、シドニーは irons in the fire をたくさん持っておくのが好きだった。
Sidney liked to keep many irons in the fire until he had a nervous breakdown.

### odds are (that)
to have a good chance that something will become true.
〜の可能性が高い；きっと〜の可能性が高い。

odds are、帰る頃にはラスベガスへ持って来たお金はなくなっているだろう。
Odds are that the money you bring to Las Vegas will be gone when you return.

### fight a losing battle
to attempt to do something with no chance of success.
見込みのない戦いをする。

バリーは3年間、癌と fight a losing battle してから亡くなった。
Barry fought a losing battle with cancer for three years before he finally passed away.

## pass up

to refuse, reject or turn down an opportunity.
～を断る；(食べる・見る)機会を逃す。

レスリングしていた時、痩せるために私はとても美味しい料理をよく pass up しなければならなかった。

When I was a wrestler, I often had to pass up delicious food to lose weight.

## miss the boat

to lose an opportunity to do something by being slow to act.
好機を逸する；チャンスを逃す；要点をつかみ損なう。
*Synonym miss the bus.

マイクロソフトに関して私は miss the boat した。株はただひたすら上がって行く。

I missed the boat on Microsoft: their stocks just keep going up.
*Usually used for opportunities that will not come again.
(通常、二度とない機会を言う時に使います。)

## long shot

something that is highly unlikely to succeed, but worthy of an attempt; an effort or guess that has a remote chance of success.
(競馬の)大穴；当て推量；一か八かの大ばくち。

競馬場でマットはいつも long shot に賭ける。

Matt always bets on the long shot at the racetrack.

## a sure thing

something that is certain to happen or be successful.
確実なこと；疑いないこと。

ピーターはもっと用心深い。a sure thing にしか賭けない。

Peter is more careful. He only bets on a sure thing.

Risk & Reward

# Fill in the blanks with the appropriate idioms.

**01** Colonel Peterson was offered a promotion if he stayed for another tour in Korea during the war, but he _____ it _____ to return home and retire.
戦争中に韓国に残って、外国勤務をもう１期務めればピーターソン軍長は昇進出来たが、断って故国へ帰って退役した。

**02** Everyone knows that nothing is a _____ _____ when gambling is involved.
賭博のことになると確実なことはないと皆、知っている。

**03** Whenever I think about going on a trip, _____ _____ that I've been working too much.
私が旅行へ行くことを考えている時は、仕事をし過ぎている可能性が高い。

**04** Odds _____ that if you risk all of your money on a long shot, you will lose it.
大ばくちにお金を全部賭けると、失くす可能性が高い。

**05** Leanne _____ the _____ on an excellent business opportunity.
立派な仕事の好機をレアナは逃してしまった。

**06** The weather _____ kind of _____ in summer. It's as likely to pour as to shine at any time.
夏の天気はなんだかあやふやだ。雨が降る可能性も晴れる可能性も同じぐらいだ。

**07** Amy is an independent woman. It's _____-_____ that she likes to pay for dates herself.
エイミーは独立した女性だ。デートの時、彼女は自分でお金を出したいと思うか思わないかは五分五分。

**08** When Darryl applied for the scholarship, he knew it was a long _____, since so many other people were applying.
ダリルは奨学金に応募した時、他にたくさんの人も応募していたので大ばくちだと分かっていた。

**09** In order to _____ a _____ with a woman like that, you have to be bold and charismatic as well as rich and successful.
そのような女性と付き合う可能性が欲しいなら、金持ちで成功している上に大胆でカリスマ性も持っていないといけない。

**10** Sally has so many _____ in _____ _____, she often has to skip meals or lose sleep.

あまりにも多くの企画を同時進行しているので、サリーはしばしば食事を抜いたり、睡眠時間を減らしたりしないといけない。

**11** In Harrison Ford's early days as an actor, he was told that becoming famous was just a _____ _____.

俳優を始めた当時、ハリソン・フォードは有名になるなんてただの夢想だと言われた。

**12** The Johnsons tried everything to get rid of the ants in their house, but they were _____ a _____ _____.

家の中の蟻を駆除するためにジョンソン一家は全てを試みたが、見込みのない戦いだった。

**13** If you _____ all _____ _____ in one _____, you could easily lose everything. You've got to diversify your investments.

資金を全部同じものに賭けると簡単に全てを失いますよ。投資を分散させないといけない。

**14** Even though Anne sometimes _____ _____ _____ good investments, she has also made some money in the stock market.

アンは時々良い投資を見逃すことはあるにしても、株式市場で儲けたこともある。

**Answers** 1. passed (it) up  2. (a) sure thing  3. chances are  4. (Odds) are  5. missed (the) boat  6. is (kind of) iffy  7. fifty-fifty  8. (long) shot  9. stand (a) chance  10. irons (in) the fire  11. pipe dream  12. fighting (a) losing battle  13. put (all) your eggs (in one) basket  14. misses out on

# Read the following story and refer to the questions below.

**- This, That and the Other Thing**

"So Sally, have you applied to any universities yet?" asked Will. "You don't want to *miss out on* a good opportunity by delaying." "I know," said Sally. "It's a bit of a *long shot* that I'll get into my dream school, Georgetown, but don't worry: I'm not going to *miss the boat*, so I applied to a few places. I *stand a good chance* of getting accepted to at least one of my top schools, and odds are that I'll get into Berkeley since my uncle works there. It's only *fifty-fifty* that I'll get into Yale though, and a *pipe dream* to think that I'd get that scholarship to Oxford, but you never know unless you try."

"What about you? Still working too much aren't you? I remember, you always had too many balls in the air."

"Yeah, well I've got a few irons in the fire. I'm writing my book and working for the government part-time as a technical advisor, plus I still have to finish my dissertation* on Korean-Chinese business relations and of course practice judo. There are too many good opportunities out there to pass up and I don't want to put all my eggs in one basket, so I always take on new projects. Sometimes I feel like I'm fighting a losing battle, but chances are that one day all my hard work will really pay off."

*dissertation 論文；修士論文；卒業論文。

## Questions about the story

**1.** What should Sally not miss out on? Will she miss the boat?
**2.** Where does she want to go? What are her chances of getting in?
**3.** What school does she have a good chance of being accepted to? Why?
**4.** What is her pipe dream?
**5.** Does Will have many balls in the air? What are they?
**6.** Why does he do so many things?
**7.** What does he hope his chances are?

## Questions for discussion

**1.** Did you apply to many universities? What were your first choices? Why?
**2.** Is it normal to have many irons in the fire in your country?
**3.** If you could do several things, what would they be? How would you keep all the balls in the air?
**4.** Do you believe in diversification, or putting all your eggs in one basket?
**5.** Did you ever feel like you were fighting a losing battle?

### それと、あれと、後もう一つも

「それで、サリー、大学の願書は出したか？」とウィルは聞いた。「君も遅れて良いチャンスを見逃したくはないだろう？」「わかっているわ」とサリーは言った。「第一志望のジョージタウンに受かるチャンスは少し低いけど、心配しないで。好機を見逃さないようにいくつか願書を出しているわ。行きたい大学のうちの1校には合格する可能性はあるし、しかもその上に叔父がバークレーで働いているからそこに受かる可能性は高いわ。イェールに合格する可能性は五分五分だし、オックスフォードへの奨学金がもらえるのは当て推量だけど、やってみないとわからないじゃない」。
「あなたは？まだ働き過ぎているんでしょう？あなたがいつも同時にたくさんのことをしようとし過ぎていたのを覚えているわよ」。「そうだね、まぁ、いくつかの仕事はやっているよ。本を書きながら、非常勤で政府の技術アドバイザーをしている。あっ、後それに韓国と中国間の取引関係についての修士論文も書いているし、柔道の練習も当然しているよ。見逃せない素敵な機会があり過ぎて、その上に全部を一つに賭けたくはないので、いつも新しい仕事を引き受けているんだ。時々勝ち目のない戦いをしているように感じるけど、きっといつか僕の努力の成果は本当に報われるだろう」。

# 15 Getting Involved
参加する

**show up**
to appear or to be present in order to participate.
出席する；参加する；顔を出す。

来週の会議におよそ30人が show up すると期待されている。
About thirty people are expected to show up for the conference next week.

**sit out**
to not participate in an activity.
参加しない；(ダンスや競技に)加わらない。

そのバスケットボール選手は、脚の怪我のせいで試合に何回も sit out しなければならなかった。
The basketball player had to sit out of several games due to a leg injury.

**left out**
not included.
疎外感を味わう；はみだされる；仲間はずれになる。

家族で一番若かったため、ニックは家族間の話でよく left out な気分になった。
Being the youngest family member, Nick often felt left out at family meetings.

**team up (with)**
to work together to accomplish the same goal.
チームを組む；何かをするために一緒に働く。

普段は一緒に仕事をするのは好きじゃないが、新製品の売り出しに向けてサムとマイクは team up する。
Although they usually don't like to work together, Sam and Mike will team up to launch the new product.

102　Taking Action

**look on**
to watch others participate; to be a spectator or witness.
見学する；傍観する。
*Noun* onlooker
傍観者；見物人。

この会議に look on するだけなの、それとも参加するの？
Are you going to just look on, or are you going to participate in this meeting?

**take part in**
to participate in or join in; to become involved in or enter into.
参加する。
*Synonym* be in on.

今度の土曜日の営業セミナーに サリーが take part in するか分かりますか？
Do you know if Sally will take part in the sales seminar next Saturday?

**count someone in**
to be a part of; to include someone in a plan.
仲間に入れる；(予定や企画に)参加するものと考える。

来週の日曜日に浜辺へ行く予定なら、count me in して下さい。
If you plan on going to the beach next Sunday, please count me in.

**count someone out**
not to be a part of; to exclude (oneself) from a plan.
仲間に入れない；予定や企画に参加しないものと考える。

来週の日曜日に、浜辺の代わりに博物館に行くのなら、count me out して下さい。
If you are going to go to the museum next Sunday instead of going to the beach, please count me out.

**join in**
to participate or involve oneself in something (often followed by "on").
積極的に参加する；自ら何かに関わる。

マイケル、ずっととても静かにしているけど、私達と一緒にこの会議に join in しませんか？
Michael, you have been very quiet... would you like to join in on this meeting?

**have a hand in**
to play a role in; to be actively involved in.
〜に関わる；〜に影響を及ぼす。

社員を雇用する時でも解雇する時でも、部長なら誰でもその判断に have a hand in することが重要だ。
It is important for all managers to have a hand in decisions to hire or fire an employee.

# Fill in the blanks with the appropriate idioms.

**01** Sam had to _____ _____ the soccer game because he injured his left ankle in the game last week.
先週の試合で左足首を怪我したので、サムはサッカーの試合に参加できなかった。

**02** I think that Mary had a _____ _____ getting me fired from my job. She never really liked me.
私が仕事を首になったことにメリーは関わったと思う。彼女はずっと私のことがあまり好きではなかった。

**03** Our department might have to _____ _____ with the sales team to launch the next big project at work.
次の大規模なプロジェクトを立ち上げるため、私達の部署が営業部とチームを組まないといけないかもしれない。

**04** It bothers me when some members of our team choose not to _____ _____ on meetings at work and contribute.
チームの仲間が会社の会議に積極的に参加しないで、何も貢献しようとしないのが僕を困らせる。

**05** Sandra said that if we were going to the beach this weekend to _____ her _____, because she has already finished all of her homework and wants to relax.
サンドラはもうすでに宿題を全部終えてリラックスしたいから、今週末浜辺へ行くなら仲間にいれて欲しいと言った。

**06** Sandra also said that if we were planning on inviting Mark to the beach, to _____ her _____ because she and Mark don't get along.
もしマークも浜辺へ誘う予定なら、サンドラは、マークとあまり仲良くないから、参加しないとも言った。

**07** Mr. Marentette said that fifteen children are expected to _____ part _____ the school talent show next week.
来週の学校の学芸会に15人の子供の参加が期待されているとマレンテット先生が言った。

**08** Chris didn't _____ _____ for school today. He must be sick.
今日、クリスは学校に顔を出さなかった。きっと風邪を引いているのだろう。

**09** Jake's younger brother Mark was often _____ out when Jake's friends came over to the house.
ジェークの友達が家に来ると、弟のマークはよく仲間はずれにされた。

**10** It was a shame that so many people chose to _____ _____ instead

104  Taking Action

of helping the car accident victims. Onlookers at an accident are never welcome.
あれほど多くの人が、交通事故の被害者を手伝わないで、傍観していたのはとても残念だ。事故現場では見物人が歓迎されることは絶対にない。

**Answers** 1. sit out  2. (had a) hand in  3. team up (with)  4. join in  5. count (her) in  6. count (her) out  7. take (part) in  8. show up  9. left (out)  10. look on

# Read the following story and refer to the questions below.

## - Abuse of Power

When any study proposal* came across Aaron's desk, he would always weigh* his options carefully. If, by completing the study, Aaron might further his career and get the results published, he would always **take part in** it. He made sure not to **be left out** of any exciting study.

If Aaron thought that the study would lead nowhere, he would **sit out** and let some of the graduate students work on it together. Aaron was a shrewd* scientist. He would often just **look on** all of the studies and experiments that were taking place in his lab. When any study that he was not involved in began to get extra attention from the academic world, Aaron would just **show up** in the lab more regularly to check on the study in progress. Usually when most of the work was done, Aaron would find a way to **have a hand in** the study results.

As a rule, any time a senior scientist **teamed up with** graduate students for all or a part of a study, their name would be first on the published article. Most graduate students did not think this was fair, but they knew that once they became senior scientists, they would enjoy the same benefits.

*proposal 提案；プロポーザル  *weigh 量る；量り比べる  *shrew ずる賢い；如才

## Questions about the story

**1.** What type of experiments did Aaron take part in? Why?
**2.** What types of studies did Aaron chose to sit out of?
**3.** What kind of a scientist was Aaron?
**4.** What would Aaron do if the academic world gave attention to a study that he was not involved in?
**5.** What would happen every time a senior scientist would team up with a graduate student?
**6.** Is it fair when Aaron teams up with grad students near the end of a study?

## Questions for discussion

**1.** Do you like to team up with other people to complete assignments at work or school? Why or why not?
**2.** Tell me a time when something successful happened and you had a hand in it.
**3.** Have you ever had to sit out of a game or sport due to a physical condition?
**4.** When your friends make plans to go out for an evening, do they usually count you in or do you have to ask to be included?
**5.** Are you the type of person that likes to join in on interesting conversations that others are having?
**6.** What was the latest that you have ever shown up for an appointment?

---

地位の悪用

どんな研究案でもアーロンの机に届いた時は、いつもオプションをじっくり計り比べて選択をした。もし、研究に参加することで、自分の職歴をさらに進めて、結果を出版できそうだと思ったらいつも参加するようにしていた。面白そうな研究からは絶対に仲間はずれにされないようにしていた。

研究はどこにも行き着きそうにないと思ったら、参加しないで、院生の何人かにそれを担当させた。アーロンはずる賢い科学者だった。多くの場合は自分の実験室で行われている実験や研究をただ傍観していた。彼が関わっていない研究が学界から注目を浴び始めたら、アーロンは、その研究の進行を観察するために、もう少し頻繁に実験室に顔を出した。普段は、研究がほとんど終わっている時点で、研究の結果に何とかして関わるような手口をみつけた。

原則として、先輩の科学者が研究の全過程または一部で院生とチームを組んでいると、出版される論文には先輩の名前が先に記された。ほとんどの院生はこれを不公平と思っていたが、自分達も先輩の科学者になれば、同じ特権が味わえると分かっていた。

# Chapters 11 - 15

Review Chapters 11-15 and fill in the crossword below.

### Across

03. We all worked hard except Jimmy. He just sat there and didn't _____ _____ _____.
06. When do you think you will get _____ _____ cutting the grass? It's already a foot high!
07. I'm not sure what it's all about, but I'll _____ _____ it.
10. I just can't _____ _____ around pretty girls.
11. Forgive me. It was just a little _____ _____.
12. If you need to find Arnold, _____ _____ that he's at the gym.
14. Did you _____ _____ any mention of the Ark of the Covenant in your studies.
15. Owen Meany often felt _____ _____ in gym class because he was so small.
19. Remember, the only _____ _____ in life are death and taxes.
20. Stop _____ your _____ and get to work.
21. How can you _____ _____ a desert like this?
22. I would love to play, but I hurt my foot so I'm going to have to _____ this one _____.
23. I can't wait to _____ _____ on the fun!
24. I'm not sure where my cell phone is, but I'm sure it will _____ _____ soon.
25. Inspector Clouseau _____ _____ the Pink Panther.

### Down

01. Everybody's going up to the cabin to go fishing. Can I _____ you _____ ?
02. I've got to get it done by tomorrow, so I will have to burn the _____ _____.
04. Jeff put his _____ _____ _____ _____ so many times, his tongue must taste like toes!
05. Jill _____ _____ _____ a great idea at the meeting yesterday.
08. Sorry kid, there's no chance for a _____ _____ in life.
09. You want to fight Tyson?! You don't _____ a _____.
13. It's hard to _____ _____ with all the recent changes in technology.
16. Oops, I _____ _____ and put the wrong kind of gas in the car.
17. Don't _____ the _____ on this great opportunity.
18. Jimmy, did you have _____ _____ _____ playing a joke on your teacher?

# 16 Defense, Support & Backing

守り、援助、支援

### stand up for
to defend, support or prove someone or something right.
(人・権利などを)守る、擁護する；(誰か・何かを)支持して正しいと証明する。

職場で自分の権利のために stand up for することは大切だと思う。
I think it's important for you to stand up for your rights at work.

### come out in favor of
to reveal or state openly a favorable position.
〜を支持している態度を明らかに示す。

元大統領は選挙で負けた時、新大統領に come out in favor of した。
The former president came out in favor of the new president when he lost the election.
This idiom is used for formal support and political endorsements.
(この慣用句は公式的・政治的な支援を示す時に使います。)

### back up
to support a person or idea; to prove or confirm something.
(主張などを)証拠立てる；(人・考えを)支援する；〜を裏付ける；サポートする。

警察官の申し立てが back up 出来る目撃者が数人いた。
There were several witnesses to back up the police officer's statement.

### jump on the bandwagon
to join a cause or movement; to support someone who is already likely to win.
優勢な政党・主義・企業などの肩を持つ；時流に乗る。
*Synonym* climb on the bandwagon; hop on the bandwagon.

アメリカで多くの人が jump on the bandwagon して禁煙した。
Many people in America jumped on the bandwagon and quit smoking.

Taking Action

**ride on someone's coattails**
to use someone else's success to live an easy life.
(人に)便乗する；(誰かに)つけいる；(人の)すねをかじる。

その歌手が有名になった時、彼の友達の何人かはride on his coattailsすることが出来た。
When the singer got rich, several of his friends were able to ride on his coattails.

**paper trail**
a trail of documents showing a chronology of actions.
過去の記録；文書足跡、人の行動の証拠となる文書。

政府の役人は内密取引のpaper trailを残さないように気を付けた。
The government officials were careful not to leave a paper trail of their secret dealings.
This idiom often establishes someone's guilt.
(この慣用語は罪の証拠を表す時によく使います。)

**stand behind**
to support with a guarantee or firmly believe in someone.
(人を)支持する；〜の後ろに立つ；誰かを信じる。

良い息子は、理解が出来ない時でも、父親をstand behindする。
A good son will stand behind his father even when he doesn't understand him.
This idiom is used when someone's honesty is in question.
(誰かの信頼性が疑われる時にこの慣用句を用います。)

**not have a leg to stand on**
to have no proof or evidence of truth; to have no excuse.
(主張などの)根拠がない、証明出来ない；言い訳が出来る立場でない。

嘘でごまかそうとするのをやめなさい。君はnot have a leg to stand on！
Stop trying to lie your way out of it. You don't have a leg to stand on!

**acid test**
proof; a thorough and critical test to prove someone or something's credibility.
(人・物の価値などの)厳格な基準；試練；証拠。

キム教授の人間解剖学のクラスは全ての医師や看護師志望者のacid testだ。
Professor Kim's human anatomy class is the acid test for all would-be doctors and nurses.

**pull for**
to hope for someone or something to succeed; to cheer for; to encourage and support an effort.
(チーム・候補者などを)支持する；口添えする；〜を助ける；〜の成功を望む。
\*Synonym root for.

今度の生徒会選挙で私はあなたにpull forする。
I'll be pulling for you in the upcoming student government elections.

# Fill in the blanks with the appropriate idioms.

**01** The CIA made sure not to leave a _____ _____ that would indicate their involvement in the covert operations.

CIAは秘密作戦への関わりの証拠となるような文書を残さないように気を付けた。

**02** Don't worry: if you have trouble explaining something in the meeting, I'll _____ you _____.

会議で何かをうまく説明出来なくても気にしないで、私がサポートするから。

**03** In an oppressive society, people aren't able to _____ _____ for their rights.

非道な社会では、人々は人権を守ることが出来ない。

**04** If you need an _____ _____ of my ability to handle pressure, just put me in an impossible situation and see how I do.

私がプレッシャーに耐えられるかどうかの証拠が欲しければ、無茶な状況に置いて、私がどう反応するか見ればいいのだ。

**05** The dictator surprised the world when he _____ out in _____ of equal rights and free elections for the people.

その独裁主義者は民衆のための自由な選挙と平等の権利を支持する態度を取った時に世界中の人々を驚かせた。

**06** The workers decided to _____ _____ the company's decision to temporarily cut wages because they believed it would come back to them the long run.

長い目で見れば自分達にとっても利益となると信じて、従業員は給料の一時削減を支持することにした。

**07** Whenever I was sad or frustrated when studying abroad, I just had to remember that my family was _____ _____ me to succeed.

留学中に悲しくなったり失望したりした時は、家族が私の成功を望んでいるのだと思い出すだけで良かった。

**08** The older generation is often slow to _____ on the _____ of new ideas or customs.

昔の世代の人は多くの場合、新しい考え方や習慣の時流に乗るのが遅い。

**09** Jerry refused to ride _____ _____ _____ of his successful father. He wanted to make his own way in the world.

ジェリーは成功している父親のすねをかじることを拒否した。自分の力で出世したいと思っていた。

**10** Your Honor, the defendant was caught in the act of stealing on video. He doesn't _____ a leg _____ _____ _____.

裁判長殿、被告人が盗みを働いている瞬間をビデオが捉えています。彼は弁解できるような立場ではありません。

**Answers**  1. paper trail  2. back (you) up  3. stand up (for)  4. acid test  5. came (out in) favor (of)  6. stand behind  7. pulling for  8. jump (on the) bandwagon  9. (ride) on the coattails  10. (doesn't) have (a leg) to stand on

# Read the following story and refer to the questions below.

### - The Reporter

As a reporter for the Seattle Times, Linda had seen and heard her fair share of stories. She'd seen the people that give up everything to stand up for what they believe in when no one would stand behind them. She'd heard people scoff at* some young upstart* politician only to jump on the bandwagon pretending to cheer him just as he wins. And she'd seen the big business crooks* that would face the court saying their accusers didn't have a leg to stand on - until she dug up the paper trail to prove them wrong. But to some, her story was the most interesting.

Her father was the chief editor at the newspaper when she got the job. He had been worried that people would think Linda was riding on his coattails, so he put her to the acid test in the first year. While he was secretly pulling for her to succeed, he piled on the work. After she had earned her father's trust, he was finally able to come out in favor of her and accept her as an equal. To her, the most important and heartwarming story to discover was that he'd always been there to stand behind her, ready to back her up if she had trouble.

*scoff at 嘲笑する；〜をあざ笑う  *upstart 成り上がり者  *crook 悪者；泥棒；いかさま師；犯罪者

## Questions about the story

1. What did some people stand up for even when others wouldn't stand behind them?
2. Were the people true followers of the politician? What did they do?
3. Did the businessmen's accusers have a leg to stand on?
4. What did Linda do to prove them wrong?
5. How did she start her job as a reporter?
   What was her father worried about?
6. What was she forced to go through?
7. Was she able to finally get her father's open support? How?
8. What had her father always done?

## Questions for discussion

1. Have you ever come out in favor of an unpopular idea?
   Did anyone stand behind you?
2. What would be a good acid test for employees in your country?
3. If your friend suddenly became very successful,
   would you be willing to ride on his/her coattails?
4. What are the things you would be willing to stand up for?
5. Have you (or anyone else) ever tried to maintain a lie when you didn't have a leg to stand on?

### 記者

シアトルタイムズの記者としてリンダはさまざまな事件を目撃したり耳にしたりしていた。誰も信じてくれない時に全てを捨てて、自分の考えを死守する人達を見てきた。若手の成り上がり政治家を嘲笑しておいて、彼が勝つと、その肩を持ち声援するふりをする人の話も聞いていた。そして、彼女が悪事の証拠となる文書を掘り出すまで、裁判で原告人の証言には根拠がないと言い続ける大手企業のいかさま師も見てきた。しかし、ある人にとっては、彼女自身の話が一番興味深いものだった。

彼女が仕事に就いた時は、彼女の父親が新聞の編集長だった。リンダが父親に便乗していると思われることを気にして、最初の一年間は彼女に試練を受けさせた。影では彼女の成功を望みながら、大量の仕事を彼女に振り分けた。彼女が父親の信頼を得てから、やっと父親は彼女を支持する態度を明らかにし、対等者として見なすことが出来た。彼女にとって一番大切で心温まる話は、父親が最初からずっとリンダの後ろに立っていて、もし彼女がトラブルを起こしてもサポートを出来るようにしていたことだった。

# Sweat & Determination

**17 苦労と決意**

**knuckle down**
to apply oneself with dedication; to work hard at something.
(仕事などに)精を出す；〜を熱心に始める。
*Synonym* buckle down.

**不可能に見えても、私達はknuckle downして終えることにした。**
Even though it looked impossible, we decided to knuckle down and get it done.

**step up**
to increase in effort or speed.
より多くの精力を注ぐ；強化する；(量・度合いなと)を高める、増す、上げる、促進する、加速する。

**サッカーチームはいつも、重要な試合の前には練習をstep upしていた。**
The football team would always step up their practices before a big game.

**get down to it**
to begin working; to deal with the main concern or task.
まじめに仕事に取り掛かる；本論に入る。

**話ばかりして時間を無駄にするのを止めて、ただget down to itしなさい。**
Stop wasting time talking about it and just get down to it.

**go overboard**
to exaggerate or overreact; to go too far.
極端に走る；やり過ぎる；何かに夢中になる；深入りする。

**ラグビー選手はしばしば試合中にgo overboardして、怪我をした。**
The rugby players would often go overboard in the game and get hurt.
*'Go' is often followed by 'way' for emphasis.
(強調のため'go'の後に'way'がよく続きます。)

**follow something through**
to finish; to carry through to completion.
最後まで何かをやり通す；努力してやり抜く；(約束を)完全に果たす。

ランスは何かをすると決めたら、いつも最後まで follow it through した。
When Lance decided to do something, he always followed it through to the end.

**give it one's best shot**
to try one's hardest to succeed in a task.
精一杯頑張る；自分に出来るだけのことをする；ベストを尽くす。

勝とうが負けようが、give it his best shot することだけが大切だと彼のお父さんはいつも言った。
His dad always told him that, win or lose, it's only important to give it his best shot.

**shoot for the moon**
to aim high.
目標を高くする；不可能なものを得ようとする。
*Synonym* reach for the stars; shoot for the stars.

shoot for the moon しなかったら、いつまでたっても一番にはなれない。
If you don't shoot for the moon, you'll never become the best.

**come on strong**
to put forth a concerted, intensive effort.
強引である；むきになる；頑張る。

建設作業員は朝、よく come on strong したが、午後になるとゆっくりになった。
The construction workers would often come on strong in the morning, but slow down in the afternoon.
*Usually at the beginning of some endeavor.
通常、何らかの企て、または試みを始める時に使います。

**get one's second wind**
to become rejuvenated; to suddenly have restored energy or strength enabling one to continue a task or activity.
(仕事を続けるために必要な)元気を回復する；息づきをする、息切れした後再び元に戻って息をする。

1分だけ休ませて。そしたら get my second wind する。
Give me a minute to rest and I'll get my second wind.

#  ill in the blanks with the appropriate idioms.

**01** You've spent an hour talking about nothing; when are you going to _____ down to _____?
あなたは一時間も何も内容のないことを話した、いつになったら本題に入るの？

**02** Ken was able to reach the peak of the mountain when he finally got _____ _____ _____.
やっと元気が回復して、ケンは山頂に着くことが出来た。

**03** If John doesn't _____ _____ and get to work, he'll never get his paper done on time.
まじめに仕事に取り掛からないとジョンはいつまで経っても論文を予定通りに終えることは出来ない。

**04** OK, we're going to have to _____ up our efforts if we want to win the game.
よし、試合に勝ちたいなら、もっと頑張らないといけないぞ。

**05** Of all the competitors for the gold in the 100-meter hurdles, only one could win, but they all _____ it their _____ _____.
100メートルハードル走の出場選手のうち一人しか優勝できなかったが、全員がベストを尽くした。

**06** When the company started doing well, the owners _____ _____ with expansion and spent too much money to stay in business.
会社が成功し始めた時、経営者は拡張事業をやり過ぎて、経営難に陥る程お金を使い果たしてしまった。

**07** Jerry hated mediocrity. He'd rather _____ _____ _____ _____ and fail than not try at all.
ジェリーは平凡は大嫌いだった。全く挑戦しないより、目標を高くして失敗する方が好きだった。

**08** Lance Armstrong was one of the few bicyclists who could fall behind and still _____ on _____ at the end to win the race.
ランス・アームストロングは、遅れを取っても頑張って、最終的にレースで優勝出来る数少ない自転車競技選手の一人だった。

**09** The students began the project not knowing how hard it would be, but decided to _____ _____ _____ anyway.
課題がどれほど難しいものなのかも分からないまま生徒達は取り掛かったが、それでも最後までやり通すと決めた。

**Answers** 1. get (down to) it  2. (got) his second wind  3. knuckle down  4. step (up)  5. gave (it their) best shot  6. went overboard  7. shoot for the moon  8. come (on) strong  9. follow it through

# Read the following story and refer to the questions below.

### - Piano Man

Being a musician might seem like a fun job, but it's not an easy one. Harry realized when he was young that he had a talent for the piano, so he decided to give it his best shot. At first he had to balance school with his music, so he always felt like he was overworking himself. Often he'd go overboard, expecting too much of himself, because he thought it was necessary in order to shoot for the moon. Mostly, he'd just knuckle down and get through it a day at a time.

As soon as he graduated, he got a job as a DJ and had to work late nights. Even after a long night at the clubs, he'd get down to it, practicing and composing new jazzy tunes. He found that he could usually get a second wind at three or four AM and come on strong until well after dawn. Then he'd get a couple of hours of sleep before dragging himself into a music academy.

As his career began to take off, he decided to step up his efforts, getting low-paying gigs* in clubs and spending endless hours refining his abilities. In the end, it was a combination of his talent and his ability to follow through on his dreams that made him a famous musician.

*gigs 出演；演奏；ライブ

## Questions about the story

1. What did Harry decide to do when he learned of his talent?
2. What did he want to shoot for? How did he do it?
3. What did he have to do as a DJ? What did he do after work?
4. How did he get through the nights?
5. What did he do as his career began to take off?
6. What helped him to become famous?

## Questions for discussion

1. What advice would you give a friend that wasn't doing well in school or work?
2. Are you the type of person that follows a project through no matter how hard it is?
3. How can you get a second wind? Where does it come from?
4. Do you ever go overboard in making plans?
   What do you do when it becomes too much to handle?

ピアノ・マン

ミュージシャンは楽しい職業に見えるかもしれないが、簡単ではない。ハリーは若い時にピアノの才能を持っていることに気付き、精一杯頑張ることにした。最初は、音楽と学校を両立しないといけなかったので、常に無理をしているように感じた。高い目標を目指すのが必要だと思い、彼はしばしば自分に期待を掛け過ぎて、極端に深入りすることもあった。ほとんどの時はただ毎日を熱心に頑張るだけだった。

卒業してすぐに彼はDJの仕事に就き、夜遅くまで働かなければならなかった。クラブで夜遅くまで働いた後でも、彼は仕事熱心で、新しいジャズっぽい曲を練習したり作曲したりしていた。ほとんどの場合は朝の3時か4時に元気が回復するように感じて、夜明けを過ぎてからもまだ頑張ったのだ。そして2時間寝てから、彼は音楽専門学校へのろのろと足を運んだ。

音楽に成功し始めた時、彼はさらに精力を注ぎ、クラブで低賃金のライブをしたり、永遠と時間を掛けて、腕を磨いた。結局、彼の才能と夢を最後まで果たすための努力が合わさって彼は有名なミュージシャンになったのだ。

# 18 Wants & Needs

要望と要求

### feel like
to want to do something; to have a desire to do or have something.
〜がしたい；〜が欲しい。

ダンは体を傾けてマイクに近寄り「僕は大きなペペローニピザを食べるfeel likeだ」と言った。
Dan leaned over to Mike and said, "I feel like eating a large pepperoni pizza."

### long for
to yearn for; to wish for something that one does not have.
〜を恋しく思う；〜を欲しがる；切望する；熱望する。

軍隊に入っていた間、ニックは母の手料理をlong forした。
Nick longed for his mother's cooking while he was away in the military.

### could go for
would be happy to have; would benefit from having something; would be satisfied with.
〜があれば嬉しい；〜が欲しいと思う；〜があれば満足する。
*Synonym* could do with.

工場での長い一日が終わりジェフは笑顔で「よく冷えたビールがcould go forだ」と言った。
After a long day at work in the factory, Jeff smiled and said, "I could go for a nice cold bottle of beer."

### be dying for/to
to want to have very much; to long for/to.
〜とても欲しがる；〜を切望する；〜がしたくてしょうがない。
*Synonym* be itching for; have a hankering for.

ティムは何か食べ物にbe dying forだと言った。
Tim said that he is dying for something to eat.
*'Be dying for' is always followed by a noun whereas 'be dying to' is followed by a verb. This is an informal idiom.
('be dying for'の後には必ず名詞が続きます。これに対して'be dying to'の後には動詞が続きます。これは口語的な慣用句です。)

### have (got) dibs on
to have a first claim on something; to have priority on.
使用優先権がある；(自分が)先；(自分が)優先。
*Synonym call dibs on.

3人の友達は車へ走り、カーラは「前の席に have got dibs on だよ。」と叫んだ。
As the three friends ran to the car, Kara shouted, "I've got dibs on the front seat."
*This idiom is used to make it verbally clear that something belongs to you or that you should be the next person to use or have something.
(何かが自分の物である、または次に使うのが自分である時にこの慣用句を使って、周りにいる人に示します。)

### would rather
would prefer something; would like something better.
〜の方が良い；〜の方を好む。

アンソニーは学校へ行ってお金を使うよりも、工場で働いて貯金するほうが would rather だと両親に言った。
Anthony told his parents that he would rather work in a factory and save money than go to school and spend it.
*In this idiom 'would' often appears in the contraction form like 'I'd rather'.
(略して'I'd rather'として使うことがよくあります。)

### to each his own
everybody has their own specific ideas or preferences; "it is acceptable for people to like or believe in different things."
「人それぞれ」；十人十色；それぞれに好みがある。

自分がゲイだとマークが発表した時、多くの人は驚いたが、私は前からいつも「to each his own」と言っていた。
When Mark announced that he was gay many people were shocked, but I have always said, "To each his own."
*This idiom is always used with the possessive 'his.'
(この慣用句はいつも所有代名詞の'his'を使って用います。)

### had better
should; ought to.
〜するべきである；〜するのが良い；〜する方が良い。

昨晩、遅くまで出掛けていたから妻が怒っているので、クリスは今夜早く家に帰るのが had better だ。
Chris had better go home early tonight because his wife is angry that he stayed out the night before.
*In this idiom, a person has several choices, but should choose the most sensible one under the current conditions.
(この慣用句を使うと、たくさんの選択肢はあるがその状況で一番分別のある行動を取るべきだと言う意味になります。)

**have got to**
must; have something essential to do; be necessary to do.
〜しなければならない；〜する必要がある；必ず〜しないといけない。
*Synonym* have to.

明日のテストに合格する希望があるならサリーは一晩中勉強を have got to する。
Sally has got to study all night if she is to have any hope of passing her test tomorrow.

**be supposed to**
to be expected by others to do something; to have a responsibility or duty to do something.
〜しているはず；〜であるはず；〜することになっている；〜する必要がある。

弊社の社員は be supposed to 朝の8時半までに会社に来て働いています。
Our company employees are supposed to be in the office working before eight-thirty in the morning.

# F ill in the blanks with the appropriate idioms.

**01** Although I really can't understand why Eric bought a bright pink car, I just say to myself, " _____ each _____ _____.
エリックが何故、派手なピンクの車を買ったのか本当に理解できないが、私は「人それぞれ」だと自分に言い聞かせるだけだ。

**02** If we are going to finish this project by tomorrow, we _____ _____ _____ work all night.
明日までにこの課題を終えるつもりならば、私達は一晩中働く必要がある。

**03** Steve said that he _____ _____ eat worms than go out on a date with Sarah.
サラとデートをするならミミズを食べるほうがましだとスティーブは言った。

**04** Peter's schoolteacher told him that he _____ _____ hand in his papers on time or he could end up failing the course.
論文を時間通りに提出した方が良い、さもないと単位を落とすかもしれないと学校の先生はピーターに言った。

**05** After spending nearly his whole life in school, Jason told his family that he was _____ _____ travel around the world.
人生の大半を学校で過ごしてからジェイソンは世界中を旅することを切望していると家族に言った。

**06** Tina missed her boyfriend quite a lot, and often _____ _____ him when she was lonely.
ティナが寂しい時は、よく彼氏に会いたい気持ちになり、恋しく思った。

**07** I _____ _____ _____ a little break from my math homework. Would you like to go get some ice cream with me?
数学の宿題の合間にちょっとした休憩が欲しいわ。一緒にアイスクリームを食べに行かない？

**08** Professor Smith reminded his students that they are _____ _____ hand in their reports by next week."
スミス教授は来週までにレポートを提出する必要があると生徒に思い出させた。

**09** After eating salty potato chips, Aaron _____ _____ drinking a cola to wash away the salty taste.
塩辛いポテトチップスを食べてから、アーロンはコーラを飲んで塩っぽい味を流し去りたいと思った。

**10** Jim was so hungry that he said, "I've _____ _____ on the last piece of pizza so don't eat it."
ジムはあまりにもお腹が空いていたので「ピザの最後の一切れは僕のだから食べないで。」と言った。

Wants & Needs 121

**Answers** 1. To (each) his own  2. have got to  3. would rather  4. had better  5. (was) dying to  6. longed for  7. could go for  8. (are) supposed to  9. felt like  10. (I've) got dibs (on)

# Read the following story and refer to the questions below.

### - Weekend Conference

The last thing Gord felt like doing on the long weekend was attending a conference for work. He told his boss that he would rather let someone else take his place so he could enjoy spending the weekend with his family and friends. He was also dying to try out his new clubs on the golf course. But he thought that he had better go to the conference instead, because it's something he felt that he was supposed to do.

As he sat in the first of five workshops, he longed for the days when he could leave work on Friday and forget about it until Monday. After the morning session of meetings was complete, Gord figured he could do with a large lunch. While waiting in line with some of the other middle managers, he called dibs on the only piece of roast beef he could see. When no one seemed to argue, he served himself the last portion of meat. The manager behind Gord leaned forward and said, "Gord, you have got to have patience in the food line. They'll bring us out a fresh platter of roast beef soon enough."

Gord knew that patience was not his strongest attribute* and that maybe it would have been better if he had not come to the conference at all. Finally, he mumbled,* "To each his own" under his breath and decided to skip the rest of the conference and go golfing.

*attribute 性質；特徴；特質  *mumble ぶつぶつ言う；つぶやく

## Questions about the story

1. What was the last thing Gord felt like doing on the weekend?
2. What did he tell his boss?
3. What was he dying to do?
4. Why did Gord think he had better go to the conference?
5. What was he doing in the first of the five workshops?
6. How did he claim the last plate of roast beef?
7. What did the manager behind Gord tell him? Why did he tell him that?
8. Why did he mumble, "To each his own" under his breath?

## Questions for discussion

1. Describe something that you would least like to do on the weekend.
2. How would you rather spend your weekend?
3. Describe something that you are dying to try.
4. Share something that you have longed for and explain why.
5. Describe a situation where it is in your best interest to do what you are supposed to do.
6. When you were younger, how did you call dibs on something in your family?
7. What kind of food could you do with right now?

---

**週末の会議**

三連休の週末にゴードが一番したくないと思っていたことは仕事の会議に出ることだった。週末を家族や友達と楽しく過ごしたいので、他の誰かに代わりに行ってもらう方がいいと彼は上司に言った。それにゴルフ場で新しいクラブを使ってみたくてしょうがなかったのだ。それでも参加することになっていると思い、楽しく過ごすことより会議に行くべきであると考えた。

5つの研究会のうちの一つに参加しているときに彼は、金曜日まで働いてから月曜日までは、仕事のことを忘れられる日々を恋しく思った。朝の部の会議が終わり、ゴードは大盛りの昼食が欲しいと考えた。他の中間管理者と一緒に列に並んでから、一つしか残っていないローストビーフの一切れが自分の物であると言った。誰も反対しないようだったので、彼は最後の肉を自分のお皿に載せた。ゴードの後ろにいた部長は前かがみになり「ゴードさん、食事の列では順番を待たないといけませんよ。そのうち新しいローストビーフを出してくれますから。」と言った。

ゴードは気長に待つことは自分の長所でないと分かっていたので、最初から会議に来ない方が良かったかもしれないと考えた。結局、小声で人それぞれだとつぶやき、残りの会議をサボりゴルフをしに行くことにした。

# 19 Inquiring & Interfering

### mind one's own business
to be concerned with one's own affairs.
「大きなお世話だ」;「おせっかいはよせ」;自分のことだけを気にして、他の人のことのプライベートに立ち入らない。
*Synonym mind one's own beeswax; butt out.

離婚がどうなっているのかリンダに尋ねたら「mind your own business.」と言って睨まれた。
When I asked Linda how her divorce was going, she glared at me and said, "Mind your own business."
*This idiom is said informally to people who are interfering in someone else's business or asking an inappropriate question.
(この慣用句は口語的で、聞かれたくないことを聞かれた時やプライベートについて聞かれた時に使います。)

### get on someone's case
to pester someone about a particular issue; to criticize and pressure someone.
〜に干渉する;〜にプレッシャーを掛ける;〜を批判する。
*Synonym get on someone's back.

未完成のプロジェクトのことで、ティムの上司は get on his case し始めている。
Tim's boss is starting to get on his case about the unfinished project.

### get off someone's case
to stop pressuring and pestering someone about an issue.
〜に干渉するのをやめる;〜の邪魔をするのをやめる;〜を放って置く。
*Synonym get off someone's back.

企画について激しい口論をしてから、ティムは「get off my case」と叫んだ。
After a heated discussion about the project, Tim shouted, "Get off my case!"
*This idiom is said as a frustrated response to being pressured to do something or criticized excessively. It is informal.
(プレッシャーを掛けられている時や批判を浴びている時にイライラのこもった返事としてこの慣用句を使います。口語的な表現です。)

### get lost
to stop bothering or pestering someone by leaving; to leave someone alone.
「どっかいけ」;「邪魔するな」;「ほっといて」;「消え失せろ」。
*__Synonym__ go away; take a hike; beat it; scram; hit the road.

スティーブンが付き合って欲しいと4度目にエリカに言った時、彼女はただ「get lost」と言ってドアをバタンと閉めた。
When Steven asked Erica out for the fourth time, she just said, "Get lost!" and slammed the door.

### stick one's nose into
to purposely meddle or interfere; to be nosy.
誰かの事情に干渉する;おせっかいをする。
*__Synonym__ butt in.

ダンは他人の事情にstick his nose intoする度に問題を起こした。
Dan gets into trouble every time he sticks his nose into other people's affairs.

### be none of someone's business
to not be an issue that one should be concerned with; not one's concern.
〜が気にすることではない;〜とは関係ない;〜がそれについて聞く必要がない。
*__Synonym__ be none of someone's beeswax.

アルベートはミンディーに個人的な問題ついて聞きたいのだがbe none of his businessだと分かっている。
Albert wants to ask Mindy about her personal problem, but he knows that it is none of his business.

### busybody
a person who gossips or meddles in other's business; a nosy person.
おせっかい屋;出しゃばり屋;世話焼き。
*__Synonym__ nosy-parker, meddler.

仕事でティナはbusybodyだと言われている。よく他人のおせっかいを焼いている。
Tina is known at work for being a busybody. She is often meddling in other people affairs.

### be in the way
to be blocking someone or hamper their efforts to do something.
邪魔している;邪魔物である;妨げになっている。

家族のために夕食を作ろうとしていた時、ジュリーは夫に「あなたはbe in the wayだわ！」と怒鳴った。
Julie shouted, "You're in the way!" at her husband as she tried to cook dinner for the family.
*Possessive adjectives such as 'my' and 'your' are commonly used instead of 'the' in this idiom.
('the'の代わりによく'my'や'your'のような所有代名詞を用います。)

### knock it off
to stop an annoying action or behavior.
「やめろ」;迷惑なことを止める。
*__Synonym__ cut it out; quit it.

息子3人が居間で大きな音を立てていたのでアレックスは急ぎ「knock it off!」と言った。
Alex rushed into the living room where his three sons were making noise and said, "Knock it off!"

# Fill in the blanks with the appropriate idioms.

**01** If you _____ _____ nose _____ other people's business, you will end up causing problems.
他人におせっかいをすれば、結局、問題を起こしてしまうよ。

**02** You are not really helping me at all. Actually, you are in _____ _____.
あなたは本当に私の助けになってないのよ。本当のことを言うと邪魔なの。

**03** Cindy is a real _____. She is always gossiping and chattering about people at the office.
シンディーは本当に出しゃばり屋だ。彼女はいつも会社の人の話をしたり、噂を流したりしている。

**04** When I asked Steven and Tom why they were arguing with each other, Tom frowned at me and said, "_____ your _____ _____."
なぜ喧嘩をしているのかスティーブンとトムに聞いた時、トムは顔をしかめて「大きなお世話だ」と言った。

**05** I know that it is _____ of my _____, but why did you and Trevor break up?
私が気にするべきことではないとは分かっているが、なぜトレバーと別れたの?

**06** Every time Laura tells her younger brother to _____ _____, he makes sure not to leave until he's bored with bothering her.
ローラが弟にどっかへ行ってと言うと、弟は必ず飽きるまで彼女の邪魔をし続ける。

**07** I wish that my boss would just _____ _____ my _____ about the project at work, but he keeps on bothering me every day.
会社のプロジェクトについて上司が干渉をするのをただ止めて欲しいと思うのだが、毎日上司は私の邪魔をする。

**08** Samantha _____ _____ her husband's _____ about the mess he had left in the garage.
夫がガレージを散らかしたままにしていたことについてサマンサは彼を批判した。

**09** Bob looked at his younger brother who was playing dead on the carpet and said, "All right, _____ it _____ before I get angry."
じゅうたんの上で死んだふりをしている弟を見てボブは、「はい、もういいから、僕が怒る前に止めろ」と言った。

**Answers** 1. stick your (nose) into  2. (are in) the way  3. busybody  4. Mind (your) own business  5. none (of my) business  6. get lost  7. get off (my) case  8. got on (her husband's) case  9. knock (it) off

# Read the following story and refer to the questions below.

### - A Nosy-Parker

Michelle Parker didn't know it, but everyone in the building referred to her as the office busybody. To most people, it seemed as if she never did any work. She spent far too much time in other people's cubicles,* sticking her nose into things that didn't concern her. She had no idea that many of her friends secretly wished she would just get lost. Whenever Michelle's friends would ask her to leave so they could get some work done, she would just wave her arm at them and tell them jokingly to knock it off. She didn't understand that most people wanted her to mind her own business.

Things changed when Tom, a new employee, had asked Michelle to get off his case when she kept coming over to his cubicle and asking him personal questions. Michelle had been surprised to hear those harsh* words because she thought everyone loved having her as company. She didn't see how she could have been on anyone's case just by asking a few questions. She started to wonder if other people in the office felt the same way as Tom. Michelle finally realized that if they did all feel the same, and she had just been a nuisance* by being in their way while they were working, then maybe she had better start minding her own business.

---

*cubicle ブース；個室；仕切り；ボックス　*harsh 鋭い；厳しい；辛辣な；きつい
*nuisance 迷惑；生活妨害；迷惑行為

## Questions about the story

1. How did the other people in the office refer to Michelle?
2. What would she do when she visited the other cubicles?
3. What was the secret wish of many of her friends?
4. What did most people want Michelle to do?

**5.** What happened with her and the new employee, Tom?
**6.** What revelation did Michelle have as a result of Tom asking her to get off his case?
**7.** Describe what she decided that she had better start doing.

## Questions for discussion

**1.** Describe the actions of someone you know that is a busybody.
**2.** Describe a situation where you have stuck your nose into someone's business.
**3.** Is there someone at your school or workplace that you secretly wish would just get lost?
**4.** Have you ever had someone on your case at work or at home? What did you say?
**5.** Describe a situation where you felt you were in the way.
**6.** Have you ever asked someone to mind his or her own business?

**おせっかい屋さん**

ミシェル・バーカーは知らなかったが、そのビルで勤めている人は皆、彼女のことを事務所のおせっかい屋と呼んでいたのだ。ほとんどの人から見て彼女はいつも仕事をしていないように見えた。他人のブースへ行き、自分に関係ないことについておせっかいを焼くことにかなり時間を費やしていた。何人もの友達が彼女にどこかへ消え失せて欲しいと思っていたことを彼女は知らなかった。仕事をしないといけないのであっちへ行って欲しいと友達に言われればミシェルは手を振って、冗談半分に、止めてよ、と言った。ほとんどの人はもっと彼女に自分のことだけを気にして他人のプライベートに立ち入らないで欲しいと思っていたことを彼女は理解出来なかったのだ。

いつも自分のブースに来てプライベートな質問をするミシェルに対して、トムという新入社員が邪魔をするのを止めろと言った時から状況は一転した。会社にいる皆がミシェルに相手をしてもらえて嬉しいとミシェルは思っていたので、その厳しい言葉を聞いてミシェルは驚いた。ちょっとした質問をするだけで他人の干渉をしていたということが彼女には分かっていなかった。事務所にいる他の人もトムと同じように考えているのかなと考え始めた。もしも皆がそう言う風に考えていたとしたら、皆が仕事をしようとしている時に邪魔をしていたことは本当に迷惑だったのだと言うことにやっと気づいて、これからはもっと自分のことだけ気にした方がいいかもしれないと考えた。

# Pick & Choose

**20 選び抜く**

**pros and cons**
the arguments for and against something.
良い点と悪い点；良し悪し。

**決断をする前にpros and consについてじっくり考えなさい。**
Carefully consider the pros and cons before you make a big decision.
*Usually preceded by 'weigh' or 'consider.'
(通常、'weigh'または'consider'が前に付きます。)

**make up one's mind**
to make a final decision or resolution.
決める；決心する；最終的な決断をする。

**エベレストに登頂しようとmake up her mindした時、もう彼女を止められるものは何もなかった。**
When she made up her mind to conquer Everest, nothing could stop her.
*In this idiom, 'up' can come after 'one's mind' and 'mind' can be plural.
この慣用句では'one's mind'の後に'up'が付くことも、'mind'が複数形になることもあります。

**pick and choose**
to select carefully; to take a long time to make a choice.
〜を慎重に時間を掛けて選ぶ；(上等なものばかり)選ぶ；精選する。

**ウェンディは自分の一番好きな食べ物をpick and choose出来るから、バイキングで食べるのが大好きだ。**
Wendy loves to eat at the buffet because she can pick and choose her favorite foods.

### leave something (up) to
to give up or assign the responsibility of a decision to someone or something.
〜に何かを任す；〜に何かをしてもらう；代わり誰かに責任を受け渡す。

何を注文したらいいのか決められないので、ウェイターに leave it up to する。
I can't decide what to order, so I'll just leave it up to the waiter.

### settle on
to come to an agreement; finally decide on.
〜に決める；〜を選ぶ；〜に同意する。

お父さんに医学または法学を勉強しなさいと言われたのに、結局私は哲学を専攻することに settle on した。
My dad told me to study medicine or law, so I finally settled on becoming a philosophy major.

### rule of thumb
a common rule or guideline; a reliable method based on experience.
大雑把な方法・決まり；経験に基づく方法・決まり。

私の母の rule of thumb は、食べてから30分以内にプールで泳がないことだった。
My mother's rule of thumb was not to go swimming for 30 minutes after eating.

### take it or leave it
to accept or refuse something without change.
承諾するかしないかは君の勝手だ；〜をするかしないかは君の勝手だ；いやならやめろ。

この車は現在の状態のまま500ドルで販売しています。take it or leave it して下さい。
This car is $500 and sold as-is. Take it or leave it.
*This idiom is often used as a command.
(よく命令形で用いられます。)

### leave something open
to not make a decision about something.
〜を空けておく；〜スケジュールを決めない；選択の自由を残しておく。

いつでも手術が出来るように医者は leave his schedule open しなければならなかった。
The doctor had to leave his schedule open to be able to do surgery at any time.

### call the shots
to dominate, make decisions or control a situation.
仕切る；決断をする；決定を下す；支配する。

ここではジェリーが call the shots しているので、何をすれば良いのか彼に聞いて下さい。
Jerry's calling the shots here, so ask him what to do.

### take one's pick
to be free to choose; to select whatever one wants.
好きに選ぶ；自由に選ぶ。
*Synonym have one's pick.

コロンビア大学から経営学修士を得て卒業すれば、仕事を take your pick できる。
If you graduate with an MBA from Columbia, you can take your pick of jobs.
*This idiom is often used as a command.
(よく命令形で用いられます。)

#  ill in the blanks with the appropriate idioms.

**01** My wife is the one who _____ the _____, so she'll have to make the decision.
ここを仕切っているのは妻なので、彼女が決めなければいけないだろう。

**02** In the service industry, a good _____ _____ _____ is that the customer is always right.
サービス業界では、お客様がいつも正しいとするのは良い決まりだ。

**03** I have no idea what time I'll be done with the project to give it to you. Can we _____ the time _____ and I'll call you when I finish?
何時にプロジェクトを終えてあなたに手渡すことができるか全然分かりません。時間を決めずに、終わったら電話をするようにしてもいいですか？

**04** You'll have to do a lot of research on different universities before you can weigh the _____ _____ _____ and make your choice.
色々な大学についてたくさん調べないと、それぞれの良い点と悪い点を比べて選択することは出来ない。

**05** When Manny travels, he never has an itinerary. He just starts off and _____ the rest _____ _____ chance and fate.
マニーは旅行をする時、計画を一切立てない。まずは出発をして、その後のことは成り行きと運命に任せている。

**06** I wanted to see an action movie and she wanted to see a romance, so we finally _____ _____ the "The Spy who Loved Me."
私はアクション映画が見たかったのに対して、彼女はロマンスを見たかったので、結局「私を愛したスパイ」に同意して決めた。

**07** The bartender never had to chase women. They would come up to him and he could _____ and _____.
あのバーテンダーは決して女性を追いかけなくとも良かった。彼女達の方から彼に近寄って行って、彼は好きな女性を選べたのだ。

**08** Once he _____ up his _____ to marry her, he became more devoted and caring than ever.
彼女と結婚すると決めた時、彼はさらに優しくなり、彼女を熱愛した。

**09** After we helped repaint his house, Lance Armstrong took us out to his garage to see a bunch of bicycles and said," _____ _____ _____."

家にペンキを塗り終えた後、ランス・アームストロングはガレージへ私達を連れて行き、たくさんある自転車を指して「好きに選んでいいよ。」と言った。

**10** Sorry, this is not a negotiation. Your allowance is $10 a week, _____ it or _____ _____.

ごめん、これは交渉ではないの。君のお小遣いは一週間に10ドルだ。嫌なら貰わなくてもいいのよ。

**Answers** 1. calls (the) shots  2. rule of thumb  3. leave (the time) open  4. pros and cons  5. leaves (the rest) up to  6. settled on  7. pick (and) choose  8. made (up his) mind  9. take your pick  10. take (it or) leave it

# Read the following story and refer to the questions below.

### - True Love

"Never get involved in a land war in Asia" is a good **rule of thumb** from a great movie called The Princess Bride. In it, a young man **makes up his mind** to marry his true love, a young farm girl, but has to go into the world to make his fortune* to do it. As a poor farm boy, he cannot **pick and choose** his job, and so **leaves his future open** to chance. Fate makes him an infamous* pirate captain.

When his young maid* is kidnapped, he rescues her by fighting three men, but is then chased by an evil prince who wishes to marry and then kill her. He considers the **pros and cons** of going into the fire swamp to escape, and finally **settles on** its dangers. On the other side they are captured. In the dungeon*, he isn't able to **call the shots**, so he has to **leave his fate up to** his friends.

He is nearly dead when they rescue him, and they have to storm the castle to save his true love. It seems like suicide, and they have no choice but to **take it or leave it**. They win the battle by using their wits and a wheelbarrow* to save the girl. Finally, she is able to **take her pick** of men and chooses her true love. Then they kiss.

*make a fortune 一財産を作る；お金を儲ける  *infamous 不名誉ない；いまわしい；悪名の高い；名うての
*maid 乙女；少女；処女  *dungeon 土牢；地下牢；天守閣  *wheelbarrow 手押し車

## Questions about the story

1. What was a rule of thumb that the movie introduced?
2. What did the young man make up his mind to do?
3. Was he able to plan his future or did he leave it to chance? Why?
4. When he reaches the fire swamp, what did he settle on? How?
5. When he is unable to call the shots, what does he do?
6. When faced with the impossible task of storming the castle, do they take it or leave it?
7. What does the girl take her pick of in the end? And what do they do?

## Questions for discussion

1. Have you ever decided to leave something up to fate? How did it work out?
2. What are some good rules of thumb to live by?
3. Describe a situation where you were able to take your pick of something.
4. What are the pros and cons of living in your country?
5. Who calls the shots in your family?

### 真実の愛

「アジアでは絶対に土地争いに関わってはいけない。」これは「王女の結婚」と言う素晴らしい映画から学べる決まりだ。映画では、若い男性は心から愛している農家の少女と結婚したいと心に決めるのだが、そうするには出世して一財産を築かなければならない。貧しい農家の男であり、彼は仕事を自由に選ぶことは出来ない。将来のことを決めずに運に任せた。結局、彼は悪名高い海賊船長になる運命だった。

彼の若い乙女が誘拐された時、彼は3人の男性と戦って彼女を助けたのだが、その後、少女と結婚してそしてその少女を殺したいと思っている邪悪な王子に追いかけられるのだった。炎の沼地を渡ることを考えた時、良い点と悪い点を天秤にかけて、結局、危険に立ち向かおうと決めた。しかし向こう岸についた時に彼らは捕まってしまった。地下牢では何も自分の思い通りにならず、運命を友に託した。

友達に助けられた時、彼は死に瀕していて、彼の愛する少女を助けるためにお城を強襲する必要があった。自滅をするに等しかったが、それが嫌なら諦めるしかなかった。賢明さと手押し車を使って彼らは戦いに勝って、乙女を助けた。彼女はやっと好きな男性を選べて、心から愛する彼の下へ飛び込んだ。そして二人はキスをした。

# Chapters 16 - 20

Review Chapters 16-20 and fill in the crossword below.

### Across

01. Hey, I wasn't talking to you, so just _____ your own _____.
05. Jane is so pretty that she can _____ her _____ of any man in the room.
08. I'm going to confront the boss on the issue. Will you _____ me _____?
11. I think John went _____ when he decided to swim across the Atlantic.
13. My offer is firm. It's $500 so _____ it or _____ it.
15. Do you _____ _____ a burger? I'm starving!
16. I've _____ _____ on the last piece of chocolate cake. It's MINE!
17. You _____ _____ get to work on that Economics paper. It's due Tuesday.
18. Aren't you _____ _____ be at the office today? Yeah, but I'm sick.
20. A good _____ _____ _____ in blackjack is to assume that any unseen card is an 8.
21. Mom, tell Jimmy to stop getting _____ _____ way when I'm working on the car.
22. I wish my mom would stop _____ on my _____ about getting married.
23. _____ _____ _____ Dylan! Stop poking me in the ribs or I'll knock you down.

### Down

02. Wait. I'll get my _____ _____ in a minute, and beat you in the next game.
03. You'll never win, unless you _____ _____ your efforts.
04. The CIA destroyed the evidence so they wouldn't leave a _____ _____.
06. I'm just an employee. The manager _____ _____ _____ here.
07. When Albert started a math equation, he always _____ it _____ to the end.
09. Bill _____ _____ in favor of abortion.
10. Mary had a lot of work to do, so she decided to _____ _____ and get it done.
12. I'm not sure what's good to eat here, so I'll just _____ it _____ _____ the waiter.
14. Yeah, I could really _____ _____ some fries and a shake.
16. Hey kid, we don't want you around here so just _____ _____.
18. You've got to _____ _____ for your rights.
19. We know you did it, so don't lie. You don't have a leg to _____ _____.

# Facing Danger

**21** 危険に立ち向かう

### play it safe
to be extra careful to avoid any dangerous situations.
大事を取る；用心をする；危険を冒さない。

お母さんは私に play it safe するように言うが、私は危険な人生を歩むのが好きだ。
Mom tells me to play it safe, but I like to live on the edge.

### stick one's neck out
to expose oneself to danger.
(余計なことをして・言って)自ら危ない目に会う；ボロを出す；語るに落ちる。
*Synonym risk one's neck.

信じていない理想のために私は stick my neck out しない。
I'm not going to stick my neck out for a cause I don't believe in.

### run the risk of
to be subjected to danger; to brave some known hazard.
～する危険を冒す。

入隊することで、彼は戦争へ行く run the risk of した。
Entering the military, he ran the risk of going to war.

### close call
a narrow escape from a dangerous situation; a near miss.
危機一髪。
*Synonym close shave; be too close for comfort.

私は今日、バスと close call して、はねられそうになった。
I had a close call with a bus today when it almost hit me.

### touch and go
to be in a risky, unpredictable or precarious situation.
危険；きわどい；どんな結果になるか検討が付かない；悪い結果が出そうな。

山頂まで行けるのか分からなかった。touch and go だった。
I didn't know if I could make it up the mountain. It was touch and go.

### take a chance
to voluntarily put something at risk; to rely on fortune.
〜に賭ける；危険な賭けをする；危険を冒す；運に任せる。

投資家はハイリスクな株にtake a chanceして、そのお陰で儲かった。
The investors took a chance on a high-risk stock and it paid off.

### on the line
at risk or in danger.
危険にさらされた；危ない状況に置く；〜を懸ける。
*Synonym in the line of fire; on the front line.

賭博でお金を全て失った時、彼は自分の家をon the lineにした。
He put his house on the line when he lost all his money gambling.

### throw caution to the wind
to dive in to a situation ignoring the danger; to behave or speak rashly, ignoring imminent danger.
覚悟を決める；大胆にふるまう；危険を気にしない。

自由登山はthrow caution to the windしたがる人だけに適している。
Free climbing is only for people who like to throw caution to the wind.

### tread on thin ice
to enter a dangerous situation; to be in a precarious position, causing peril.
危険を冒す；薄氷を踏む思いがある。
*Synonym skate on thin ice; tread in dangerous waters.

小僧、お前はtread on thin iceしているぞ。俺に口答えするんじゃない。
You're treading on thin ice, young man. Don't talk back to me.

### at stake
at risk to be won or lost; in a position for something to be lost or gained.
懸けられている；危険にさらされた。

この取引に私達の会社はたくさんのことをat stakeにし過ぎている。
Our company has too much at stake in this business transaction.

### the chips are down
used when a situation is critical or one is left with few options.
いざと言う時；切羽詰まったら。

the chips are downの時は、行動を起こさないと状況がひどくなるだけだ。
When the chips are down, you have to take action or it will only get worse.
*Usually used in a clause with 'when'.
(通常'when'か付く文節で用います。)

### out of the woods
out of danger.
困難を逃れて；危険から解放されて。

朝まで起きていれば、あたなはout of the woodsになる。
If you can stay awake until morning, you'll be out of the woods.

# Fill in the blanks with the appropriate idioms.

**01** The _____ _____ _____ for the British national champion with a flat tire, but he's gotten it fixed and just regained the lead.
タイヤがパンクして全英チャンピオンは切羽詰まっていたが、修理をして、今、先頭を取り戻したところだ。

**02** Little Jimmy had a _____ call with death when he fell through the ice on Cedar Lake last winter.
去年の冬に、幼いジミー君は、シーダー湖の氷が割れて水に落ちて死ぬ手前の危機一髪だった。

**03** I love my country, and I'm willing to lay my life _____ _____ _____ to protect it.
私は母国が大好きです。守るために命を掛けてもいいです。

**04** Will was the kind of guy that would _____ his _____ _____ for a friend in need.
ウィルは、助けを必要とする友達のためなら自らを危険にさらすような人だった。

**05** The world watched the situation in Iraq become more and more _____ and _____.
イラクがどんどん危険な状態になっていくのを世界中の人々は目の当たりにした。

**06** If you _____ a _____ on me, I won't let you down.
私に任せてくれれば、絶対にがっかりさせませんよ。

**07** Ken likes to watch people throw _____ to the _____ , so he always goes to see the X-Games.
ケンは大胆にふるまう人を見るのが好きなので、いつもエクストリームスポーツを見に行く。

**08** The CEO has been on vacation for too long, and now he is _____ the risk _____ losing investor confidence.
代表取締役は長い休みを取りすぎていて、今では投資家からの信頼を失う危険を冒している。

**09** Ian was often late to work and looked unkempt until he realized he was _____ on thin _____ with his boss.
上司との関係が薄氷の上を踏むような危険な状態であると気付くまで、イアンは仕事へいつも遅刻して、だらしない格好をしていた。

**10** When someone's honor is _____ _____, they will often do whatever is necessary to protect it.
名誉が懸かっている時なら人々はそれを守るためにならしばしば何でもする。

**11** Instead of betting all of his winnings on the next blackjack hand, Tom decided to _____ _____ _____ and just bet money in small amounts.

トムは勝利金の全額を次のブラックジャックの持ち札に掛けるより、用心をして、小額を掛けていくことにした。

**12** The doctors told me that my infection had cleared up and that I was _____ of the _____ and able to leave the hospital today.

感染が治まり、もう危険を逃れたので今日退院できると医者は私に言った。

**Answers**  1. (The) chips were down  2. close (call)  3. on the line  4. stick (his) neck out  5. touch (and) go  6. take (a) chance  7. (throw) caution (to the) wind  8. running (the risk) of  9. treading (on thin) ice  10. at stake  11. play it safe  12. out (of the) woods

# Read the following story and refer to the questions below.

### - Bearly Alive

Walking through the woods on a calm autumn evening, Val had his first close call with death. "It was touch and go there for a while," he said later. Val wasn't the kind of guy who could just throw caution to the wind and go on an adventure. He liked to play it safe. When he went wandering in the woods, he didn't know that he was laying his life on the line, but that day he'd have to face a grizzly bear*.

Sure he'd wandered a little farther than usual, but when he saw the kids playing, he didn't think anything of it. Then all of a sudden, he heard a roar. At first, he started climbing a tree, but then he realized the kids were skating on thin ice as he saw them throwing rocks at the grizzly. The chips were down, but he had to act. More was at stake than his own life, so he took a chance and grabbed a nearby stick to fend off* the bear. He ran over and managed to poke the bear in the eye as it was about to attack the children.

It ran away, but he abruptly said, "We're not out of the woods yet. The bear could come back and attack at any time. Let's go!"

They stayed together and hustled out of the woods. Val had never stuck his neck out before, but now he felt like a hero – and he was, but he wasn't going to run the risk of walking in those woods ever again.

---

***grizzly bear** グリズリー；ハイイログマ；(ロッキー山脈など北米西部高地にいる熊)
***fend off** 追い払う；よける；かわす。

## Questions about the story

1. What did Val experience that calm autumn day?
2. How did he talk about it?
3. What kind of guy is Val? What did he usually like to do?
4. How were the kids skating on thin ice?
5. Why did he have to act to protect the children?
6. What was at stake that made him take a chance and try to poke the bear?
7. Why did he say they weren't out of the woods yet?
8. What had he never done before? And what was he never going to do again?

## Questions for discussion

1. Are you the type of person who likes to play it safe, or do you dare to skate on thin ice?
2. In what situation would you be willing to stick your neck out for a friend?
3. What kinds of people have to throw caution to the wind every day? Could you do their job?
4. Have you or anyone in your family ever had a close call with death? Describe it in detail.
5. Describe a time where you might say, "We're not out of the woods yet."

### 熊と危機一髪の出会い

秋の静かな夕方に、森を散歩している時、バルは初めて死に直面した危機一髪な体験をした。「あの時は本当にしばらくの間どうなるか分からなかったな」と彼は思い出して言った。バルは覚悟を決めて冒険に行くような人ではなかった。用心をするタイプだった。森をぶらついていた時に命懸けのことをしているとは知らなかったのだが、その日はグリズリーと立ち向かわないといけなかったのだ。

いつもより少し遠くまで足を延ばしたのは確かだったが、子供が遊んでいたのを見たので、何とも思っていなかった。その瞬間、彼は突然動物のうなり声を聞いたのだ。最初は木に登り始めたが、子供達が熊に石を投げつけているのを見て、彼らが危険な状況にいると気付いたのだ。切羽詰っていたので、彼は何らかの行動を取らなければいけなかった。自分の命だけが懸かっていたのではなかったので、彼は危険を冒しながら、熊を追い払うために近くにある枝を拾った。彼は駆けつけて行き、熊が子供に襲い掛かる直前に熊の目を刺すことが出来たのだった。

熊は逃げて行ったが、彼は突然「まだ危険から逃れていないぞ。熊はいつでもまた戻ってきて私達を襲うかもしれない。行くぞ！」と言った。お互いから離れないようにして、彼らは森から急いで逃げた。今までバルは自らを危険にさらしたことがなかったが、今では英雄になった気分だったし、実際、彼はヒーローだったのだ。しかしもう二度と危険を冒してまであの森へは行かなかった。

# Clashes & Complaints

**22** 対立と不満

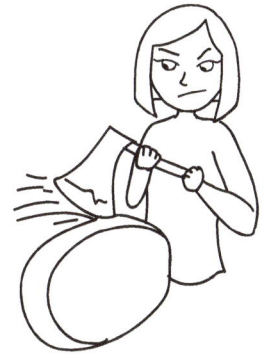

**have an ax to grind**
to have a selfish aim or personal motive for complaining or taking some action.
下心がある；腹に一物ある；不満を抱いている；自説を持つ。

有給休暇分を全額支払ってもらえなかったことで、前の雇い主にラリーは have an ax to grind した。
Larry had an ax to grind with his former employer for not receiving all of his vacation pay.

**rant and rave**
to scream and shout in anger.
怒ってわめき散らす；怒って大声を上げて叫ぶ。

ベンがお菓子を盗んで捕まった時、父は彼に向かって rant and rave した。
When Ben was caught stealing candy, his father ranted and raved at him.

**have it out (with)**
to attempt to resolve issues by way of confrontation.
〜にうっぷんを晴らす。

私の質問をいつも無視するので、近い内にいつか、あの教授と have it out with する。
One day soon, I'll have it out with the professor for ignoring my questions.

**have words (with)**
to argue or quarrel with.
〜と言い争いをする；〜と口論をする；〜と議論をする。

昇進の対象にされなかった時、メアリーは上司と have words with した。
Mary had words with her boss after she was passed over for promotion.

Clashes & Complaints  **141**

### cause a stir
to create concern or worry; to cause trouble.
混乱を引き起こす；心配をかける；騒ぎを引き起こす。

両親に遅れるという電話をしなかった時、ジェリーはかなりcause a stirした。皆とても心配していた。
Jerry caused quite a stir when he didn't call his parents and tell them that he would be late. Everyone was really worried.
*In this idiom 'quite' or 'big' are often inserted after 'cause' for emphasis.
(強調のため'quite'や'big'がよく'cause'の後に入ります。)

### stir up a hornet's nest
to cause trouble; to arouse or provoke someone's anger.
面倒を起こす；大勢の敵を作る；ごうごうたる非難を浴びる。

メアリーはいつも微妙な話題で口論をしてstir up a hornet's nestするので、私はもう彼女と話しません。
I don't talk to Mary anymore because she always stirs up a hornet's nest by arguing about sensitive issues.

### nitpick
to make trivial distinctions when arguing or criticizing; to quibble.
つまらないことでくよくよする；粗探しをする；どうでも良いことをしつこく言う。
*Synonym split hairs.

彼女と口論をするのは時間の無駄だ。いつもnitpickばかりしている。
Arguing with her is a waste of time. All she does is nitpick.

### make a big deal of
to exaggerate the significance of.
大騒ぎする；ささいなことを大げさに言う・見せる。
*Synonym make a mountain out of a molehill.
針小棒大；モグラ塚のことを山だと言う。

お母さんはいつもなぜ私の成績のことをあれほどmake a big deal ofしないといけないの？
Why does Mom always have to make such a big deal of my grades?
*In this idiom, 'such' is often inserted after 'make'.
(この慣用句を用いる時、'make'のあとに'such'を入れることがよくあります。)

### harp on
to nag, pester or hassle someone; to persistently ask someone to do something.
しつこく言う；〜をうるさくせがむ；〜のことをぺちゃくちゃしゃべる。

仕事、仕事って私にharp onしたら、私はただあなたの事を怒るだけで、仕事が終わらないよ。
If you harp on me about work, I'll just resent you and not get it done.

### blow the whistle
to inform on someone for doing something wrong.
密告する；ばらす；たれこむ；(人を)裏切る。
*Noun whistleblower.
(内部の)告発者；たれ込み屋；ばらす人。

若手の地方検事は政府内の汚職を blow the whistle したことで名を上げた。
The young district attorney made a name for himself by blowing the whistle on corruption in the government.

### a bone of contention
something to fight over; a reason to quarrel.
不和のもと；争いのもと。

子育ての考え方の違いは、お互いの関係の中で a bone of contention になった。
The couple's difference of philosophy in raising their children became a bone of contention in their relationship.

### rock the boat
to disturb a smooth or stable situation by creating problems.
状況にゆさぶりをかける；波風を立てる。
*Synonym make waves

ドミニックは社内のかけひきが嫌いだったので、よく rock the boat した。
Dominic didn't like office politics, so he would often rock the boat.

# Fill in the blanks with the appropriate idioms.

**01** Andy knew from experience not to _____ _____ his kids to do their homework. They knew it was important and learned to do it themselves.
アンディーは、経験から子供に宿題のことをしつこく言わない方が良いと知っていた。それが大切だと子供たちは知って、自分達からやるようになった。

**02** Pam's mother would constantly _____ about every little flaw in her life.
パムの母は人生のちょっとしたことでも、うまく行かないといつも全てに粗探しをした。

**03** The couple _____ _____ with their landlord after a leak from the floor above ruined their furniture.
上の階から水が漏れて、家具が台無しになったことで、そのカップルは家主と口論をした。

**04** If you intend to _____ it _____ with your boss over the lack of pay, be sure to record the conversation.
給料が支払われないことについて上司にうっぷんを晴らすのなら、必ず会話を録音するようにした方が良い。

**05** The angry tenant went after his former landlord with a good lawyer, because he had an _____ to _____ about the unsafe living conditions of the apartment.
怒っていた賃借者は、マンションで安全な生活が出来なかったと言う自説を持っていたので、優秀な弁護士を雇って以前の家主を訴えた。

**06** Even though I respect your views, if you continue to _____ _____ boat you'll never get ahead in business.
私はあたなの考え方は尊敬しているが、波風を立て続ければ、あなたはいつまでたってもビジネスで成功できません。

**07** The young secretary decided to _____ the _____ on the automobile manufacturer for knowingly producing unsafe child seats.
若い秘書は、安全でないと自覚しながらもチャイルドシートを製造していたことで、その自動車メーカーを密告しようと決めた。

**08** Tammy's husband would _____ such _____ _____ _____ of her obesity that she finally lost her extra weight and then got a divorce.
タミーが太っていると夫があまりにも大騒ぎするので、最終的には彼女は痩せてそして、彼と離婚した。

**09** The preacher was famous for _____ and _____ about the sins of politicians and other public figures.
その牧師は政治家やその他の著名人の罪について怒ってわめき散らすことで有名だった。

10  The small islet of Takeshima became a _____ _____ _____ between Korea and Japan.
竹島と言う小さな島は韓国と日本の間で争いのもととなった。

11  The Johnson's daughter _____ quite _____ _____ when she dropped out of college and went to live with her boyfriend in the wilderness.
ジョンソン家の娘が大学を中退して、彼氏と一緒に荒れ地に住みに行った時、大騒ぎを引き起こした。

12  The opening of a new bathhouse in a residential neighborhood _____ up a _____ _____ that led to angry protests at City Hall.
住宅街に新しい銭湯を開くことはごうごうたる非難を浴び、市役所の前でのデモを引き起こした。

**Answers**  1. harp on  2. nitpick  3. had words (with)  4. have (it) out (with)  5. (had an) ax (to) grind  6. rock the (boat)  7. blow (the) whistle (on)  8. make (such) a big deal (of)  9. ranting (and) raving  10. (a) bone of contention  11. caused (quite) a stir  12. stirred (up a) hornet's nest

## Read the following story and refer to the questions below.

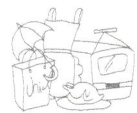

### - Web of Lies

John woke up in a sweat nearly every night since he'd **had words with** his best friend. He'd finally **had it out with** Steve about his lies. He'd even said that he would **blow the whistle on** him if he continued, but now all John could think about was that he might end his friendship with Steve if it became **a bone of contention** for him.

In the argument, Steve had gone on **ranting and raving** about John **splitting hairs** and **harping on** him about something so unimportant. "How can you **make such a big deal of** a few white lies?" Steve shouted. "Do you have **an ax to grind** with me, or something?" He **caused quite a stir** at the restaurant.

Maybe John shouldn't have **rocked the boat** when Steve was so sensitive, but he firmly believes that honesty is the best policy. John had no idea it would **stir up such a hornet's nest**. He's always complaining about his wife's **nitpicking** and the fact that she couldn't understand his friendship with his ex-wife. He wasn't doing anything wrong, just talking to her – and hiding it from his new wife.

John really didn't mean to cause such a mess, but as Sir Walter Scott put it best: "What a tangled web* we weave, when first we practice to deceive."

*tangled web 絡み合ったもの

## Questions about the story

1. Why did John wake up in a sweat?
2. What did he say to Steve? What could it become?
3. In the argument, how did Steve respond?
4. What happened when Steve started ranting and raving at the restaurant?
5. What stirred up the hornet's nest?
6. Why was he lying to his wife? What was he trying to avoid?
7. What did John not mean to do? How did he explain his feelings?

## Questions for discussion

1. What would you do if you had to face someone that was ranting and raving at you in a public place?
2. Have you ever had an ax to grind with someone? How did it work out?
3. What is the attitude in your society about blowing the whistle on others in politics?
4. Give an example of someone nitpicking in an argument. How would you respond to it?

### 絡み合った嘘

親友と言い争いをしてから、ジョンはほとんど毎晩、冷や汗をかいて目覚めた。スティーブが嘘を吐いていたことについてやっと彼にうっぷんを晴らしたのだ。もし嘘を続ければ、ばらすとまで言ったが、今になって、もしこれが不和のもとになれば、スティーブとの友情の終わりになるということしかジョンは考えることができなかった。

口論している時、ジョンが粗探しをしていたり、どうでもよいことをしつこく言っていると、スティーブは怒ってわめき散らした。「なぜちょっとした嘘をそんな大げさに騒ぎ立てるんだ？」とスティーブは叫んだ。「僕に対して何か不満でもあるのか？」とレストランで大騒ぎを引き起こした。

スティーブが敏感になっている時に、ジョンは波風を立てるべきではなかったかもしれないが、彼は本当のことを言うのが良いと強く信じていた。ジョンはこれほど面倒なことになるとは想像もしていなかった。妻がつまらないことでくよくよすることや、前の妻との関係を理解してくれないといつもスティーブは文句を言っている。何も悪いことはしていない、彼女と話をしているだけだ。そして、それを今の妻から隠しているだけ。本当はジョンもこんな混乱を引き起こしたいと思っていなかったが、サー・ウォルター・スコットの言葉が正に示すように：「まずは嘘を吐くことから、絡み合った陰謀が生まれるのだ。」

# Teamwork & Support

23 チームワークとサポート

**work with**
to cooperate with.
〜と協力する；〜と一緒に仕事に取り組む。

西欧の商習慣を理解していない人と work with するのはジェリーにとって難しいことだ。
Jerry finds it hard to work with people who don't understand Western business practices.

**play ball (with)**
to work together with; to collaborate with; to act as a team.
〜と協力する；〜と協同する。

クリスはホテルの企画の資金集めに投資銀行員と play ball with していた。
Chris is playing ball with some investment bankers to get money for his hotel project.

**take turns**
to alternate doing something.
交替する；交互にする。

子供達に take turns して物を分け合うことを教えるのはとても大切なことだ。
Teaching children to take turns and share things is very important.

**come together**
to collaborate; to team up; to have all the pieces fit to complete something.
和解する；集まる；協力する；団結する。

試合の前半でケンのサッカーチームは負けていたが、やっと come together して、最後に2点を決めた。
Ken's soccer team was losing the game in the first half, but they finally came together with two last-minute goals.

**pull together**
to work together as a team for a common purpose.
(仕事で)協力する；協調する；まとまる；一緒になって〜をする。

私達全員が pull together すればもっと速く仕事を終えることが出来る。
If we all pull together, we can get the job done much faster.

**bend over backwards**
to make a great effort to help.
(人のために)懸命の努力をする；最善を尽くす；大幅に譲歩する。

助けを必要としている友達を助けるために多くの人は bend over backwards する。
Many people would bend over backwards to help a friend in need.

**it takes two to tango**
you cannot act alone; the actions of two people are necessary to interact or argue.
両方に責任がある；一方だけに責任があるのではない。

it takes two to tango だから、あなたも何か悪いことをしたに違いない。
It takes two to tango, so you must have done something wrong too.

**put your heads together**
to cooperate to find a solution.
額を寄せて相談・密議する；解答策を見つけるために一緒に考える。

物理の問題を解くために学生達は put their heads together した。
The students put their heads together to solve the physics problem.

**team up (with)**
to join together with another person or group and do something.
チームを組む；〜と協力する。

北朝鮮と韓国が一緒に team up with すれば、より素晴らしい国際的な力になる。
If North and South Korea team up with each other, they will become a greater international force.

**do a favor**
to help someone or agree to their request.
誰かのお願いに応える；誰かのために何かをする；親切な行為をする；恩恵をする。
*Synonym do a good turn.

ウィリアムは芝生を刈って年寄りの隣人のために do a favor した。
William did a favor for his old neighbor by mowing his lawn.

**a real sport**
a person that does favors willingly.
公明正大な人；気さくな人。

私の犬の世話をして君は本当に a real sport だ。本当にありがとう！
You're a real sport for taking care of my dog. Thanks a lot!

**go out of one's way**
to do more than is usual.
(する必要がないのに)わざわざする；無理して〜をする；普段以上に〜をする。

**ケンに go out of your way して優しくして下さい。奥さんが彼を捨てて家から出て行ったばかりなので。**
Please go out of your way to be nice to Ken. His wife just left him.

# Fill in the blanks with the appropriate idioms.

**01** Remember _____ _____ two _____ _____, so we'll never agree if you're not willing to compromise.

両側に責任があることを覚えておいて欲しい。だからあなたが妥協したくないならいつまで経っても同意できませんよ。

**02** Following the hurricane, the community pulled _____ to commiserate and rebuild.

ハリケーン後にその地域の人々はお互いに哀れみ、再建に取り組んだ。

**03** To get ahead in politics, you have to _____ _____ with the business leaders.

政界で成功するにはビジネス界のリーダーと協同する必要がある。

**04** I understand that siblings disagree sometimes, but I just want you kids to _____ _____ and stop fighting.

時々兄弟は意見が対立するのは分かっているが、君達にただ仲直りして喧嘩を止めて欲しいのよ。

**05** Any time you have a problem you can't solve, it's best to call a friend and _____ your _____ _____.

解決出来ない問題がある時はどんな時でも友達に電話をして一緒に考えるのが一番だ。

**06** Jeff and his wife _____ _____ taking care of their daughter, so they can each have a night out with friends once a week.

お互いが週に一度、夜に友達と出掛けられるように、ジェフと妻は交替で娘の世話をしている。

**07** Don't worry about work while you're gone. I asked John to take care of things and he agreed. He's _____ real _____.

図がいない間の仕事のことは気にしなくていいですよ。ジョンに頼んだら良いと言っていました。彼は本当に気さくな人です。

**08** _____ _____ me rather than against me and the world can be ours.

私と対立しないで一緒に仕事に取り組めば、世界は私達のものだ。

**09** Every actor and actress should _____ _____ with a good manager to be successful.

成功をするには俳優も女優も皆良いマネージャーとチームを組むべきだ。

**10** I know Matt would _____ _____ _____ to help a friend in trouble. It's just the kind of person he is.

マットは困っている友達を助けるためなら懸命の努力をすると私は知っている。彼は単にそういう人なのだ。

**11** Even if you have to _____ _____ of your _____, I want you to find the man who did this and kill him!

無理してでも、これをやった人を見つけて、そいつを殺して欲しい！

**12** Would you _____ me _____ _____ and close the windows before you leave? It might rain tonight.

帰る前に窓を閉めてくれるようお願いしてもいい？今夜は雨が降るかもしれない。

**Answers**  1. it takes (two) to tango  2. (pulled) together  3. play ball (with)  4. come together  5. put (your) heads together  6. take turns  7. a (real) sport  8. Work with  9. team up (with)  10. bend over backwards  11. go out (of your) way  12. do (me) a favor

# Read the following story and refer to the questions below.

## - Tackling the Problem

My dad always said that *it takes two to tango*… but he wasn't there when the fight happened. It all started out with an old group of friends *coming together* to play touch football\* in the fall. We had *put our heads together* in university to do projects on economics and became closer and closer over the years, *pulling together* in hard times to help each other out. You could say we were a very tight-knit\* group.

Well, several of my friends are investment bankers and Ken, this guy I had *worked with* to do a story over the summer, kept telling me he wanted to *team up with* them. Ken said, "If you want to *play ball with* the big boys, you've got to have lots of investment capital." Somehow I felt like *going out of my way* to help him, and decided to introduce him at our weekly game since he *did me a favor* over the summer. Ken had been *a real sport* with finding people to interview about the political crisis in the White House, so I owed him a favor.

Teamwork & Support

To everyone's surprise, he started viciously* tackling people instead of just playing touch football. We tried to ignore it, but he just got worse and worse. When he hurt Jimmy, everybody just started pushing him and told him to go away before we take turns beating him. He finally left after some angry words. I had bent over backwards for him, but now I was ashamed to know him.

*touch football タッチフットボール(タックルの代わりにタッチする簡易型アメリカンフットボール)
*tight-knit 緊密な；親密な；密接な  *viciously 凶暴に；暴力的に；荒々しく；意地悪く

## Questions about the story

1. What kind of game do the people come together to play? When?
2. Where did they become friends? And how?
3. What kind of group were they? How did they become that way?
4. What do his friends do? What does the writer do?
5. What did Ken do for him? What does he say he wants?
6. Why did the players ask Ken to leave? What did they threaten to do?
7. How does the writer feel after bending over backwards for Ken?

## Questions for discussion

1. Does it take two to tango? Why or why not?
2. What does it take to play ball with the big boys in business?
3. Have you ever gone out of your way to help someone? Why and how?
4. If you do a favor for a friend and he/she does something shameful, what would you do and how would you feel?
5. What things do you do that involve pulling together as a team?

### 問題にタックルする

責任は両側にあるとお父さんはいつも言っていたが…喧嘩が起こった時、そこに彼はいなかった。秋にタッチフットボールをするために旧友が集まったことで全ては始まった。大学では経済の課題を一緒に考えて、時間が経つにつれ段々仲良くなり、辛いときにはお互いを助け合うために協力をした。とても親密な仲間だったと言える。
ところで、私の友達の多くは投資銀行に勤めていて、夏に協力して記事を一緒に書いたケンと言う人物が、彼らとチームを組みたいと言い続けていた。「社会の有力人物と協同したいのなら投資資本がたくさん必要になるだろう。」とケンは言った。なぜか私はわざわざ彼を手伝いたいと感じたのは、夏に私のお願いに応えてくれたからで、毎週行われる試合に彼を連れて行くことにした。ホワイトハウスで政治危機についてのインタビューに答えてくれる人を探してくれて、本当に気さくな人だったのでケンに恩返しをしたかった。
全員が驚いたことに、彼はタッチフットボールをするのではなく凶暴にタックルし始めた。無視しようとしたかどんどんひどくなっていった。ジミーを怪我させた時、皆で彼を押し始めて、僕たちが交替々々に殴る前に帰れと彼に言った。怒りの言葉を発してから彼はやっと帰って行った。彼のために懸命に努力をしたのに、今では彼の知り合いであることが恥ずかしく思える。

# Aptitude & Ability

**24 才能と能力**

**be all thumbs**
to be clumsy and awkward.
不器用な。

イアンは新しいコピー機を使う時**be all thumbs**で、いつも紙を詰まらせて、そこら中にインクをこぼす。
Ian is all thumbs when using the new photocopier, always getting paper jams and spilling ink everywhere.

**be cut out for**
to have the required skill or ability for.
〜に適している；〜に必要な才能・能力を持っている。

父は私に弁護士になって欲しいと望んでいるけれど、法科大学院に私は**be cut out for**でないとただ単に思う。
Although my father wants me to become a lawyer, I just think that I am not cut out for law school.
*This idiom is most commonly used in the negative form.
(この慣用語は否定文で用いることが多いです。)

**be right up one's alley**
for an activity to appropriately match or suit someone.
(人の)の能力・好みに合っている；お手のものである。

クレアは25年間、地元の警察官として勤めていたので、カジノの警備官長としての新しい仕事は**be right up his alley**だった。
Since Clare had served twenty-five years as a local police officer, his new job as head of security for the casino was right up his alley.

Aptitude & Ability 153

### have a (real) knack for
to have a special talent for something; to be naturally good at something.
〜の才能を持っている；〜が自然とよく出来る；〜を得意とする。

シンディーの母はいつも娘が演説にhave a knack forだと前から言っていた。
Cindy's mother has always said that Cindy has had a knack for public speaking.

### know something/someone like the back of one's hand
to know (a place) very well.
とてもよく知っている；(場所・物事などを)熟知している。

ニューヨークで迷子になることを気にしなくていいよ。なぜなら私がknow it like the back of my handだから。
There's no reason to worry about getting lost in New York because I know it like the back of my hand.

### have a green thumb
to be talented at gardening.
庭いじりが得意である；園芸の才能を持っている。

私の義理の母はかなりhave a green thumbだ。家の中は青々と元気に茂っている植物で溢れている。
My mother-in-law has quite a green thumb. Her house is filled with heathy, lush, green plants.

### get the hang of
to gain an understanding of how to do something.
〜のやり方を理解する；(仕事などに)慣れてこつを掴む。
*Synonym get the feel for.

２週間の厳しい研修の後、ティムは新しい仕事をやっとget the hang ofしたように感じた。
After two weeks of hard training, Tim felt that he had finally gotten the hang of his new job.

### lose one's touch
to no longer do something as skillfully as one could before.
〜才能を失う；〜が前みたいに上手に出来なくなる。

練習をしなくなり、ナタリーは年を取るにつれピアノを弾くことにlose her touchした。
As Natalie grew older, she didn't practice and slowly began to lose her touch at playing the piano.

### wet behind the ears
new and inexperienced; being a novice.
未経験な；初心者である；未熟な；青二才。
*Synonym a greenhorn.

ジェイソンのバスケットボールチームはほとんどの選手がまだwet behind the earsだったために完全に打ちのめされた。
Jason's basketball team suffered a terrible defeat because most of the players are still wet behind the ears.

# Fill in the blanks with the appropriate idioms.

**01** The novice pipefitter made many mistakes during his first month at work because he was _____ _____ the _____.
未経験だったため、その配管工は仕事を始めてからの最初の1ヶ月間は多くの間違いをした。

**02** Aunt Sally has a _____ _____. She is always tending to a plant when we visit her.
サリーおばさんは庭いじりが得意だ。私たちが訪ねるといつも植物の世話をしている。

**03** Terry thinks that it will take about a month for him to get _____ _____ of his new job, because there are so many things for him to learn.
新しく学ばないといけないことがたくさんあるので、新しい仕事に慣れるまで1ヶ月ぐらいは掛かるとテリーは思っている。

**04** Eric seems to _____ a real _____ for computer programming. He can create some programs in half the time that others can.
エリックは本当にコンピュータープログラミングの才能を持っているようだ。プログラムによっては他の人に比べて半分の時間で書くことが出来る。

**05** Judy is _____ _____ in the morning. She can't seem to pick up or hold anything without dropping it first.
朝、ジュディーは不器用だ。物を落とさずには、拾ったり持ったり出来ないようだ。

**06** After two years of not playing at a competitive level, the former pro basketball player seems to have _____ _____ touch.
2年間もの間、競技レベルの試合をしなかったことで、元プロバスケット選手は才能を失ってしまったみたいだ。

**07** I know my old neighborhood _____ _____ back _____ _____ _____.
昔の地元を熟知しています。

**08** After a few long weeks at the automotive factory, Philip realized that he was not _____ _____ _____ manual labor and decided to go back to school.
自動車工場に勤めて長く感じた数週間後、フィリップは肉体労働に自分は適さないと気付き、復学することに決めた。

**09** Jamie thought that since he played ice hockey for so many years, that rollerblading would be _____ _____ his _____.
何年間もアイスホッケーをやっていたので、ローラーブレードはお手の物だとジェイミーは思っていた。

Aptitude & Ability

**Answers** 1. wet behind (the) ears  2. (has a) green thumb  3. (get) the hang (of)  4. have (a real) knack (for)  5. (is) all thumbs  6. lost his (touch)  7. (know my old neighborhood) like the (back) of my hand  8. (was not) cut out for  9. (be) right up (his) alley

# Read the following story and refer to the questions below.

### - Backhoe Alley

T.J. had been told that one of the ways to lead a happy life is to turn your hobby into your job. He had played with toy trucks and backhoes* ever since he could remember, and he had a knack for using large machinery. His father owned a backhoe and had spent many hours showing T.J. how it worked.

It was no surprise to his parents that his first job was on one of his father's construction sites because it was right up T.J.'s alley. He started out being an assistant and using a regular shovel wherever he was needed. This was how the younger workers were supposed to learn. The older workers thought most younger workers were too wet behind the ears to get on a machine right away. While he was growing up, T.J. had heard about other young assistants who were not cut out for work on the big machines. His dad would come home from the construction sites with stories of young workers who were all thumbs and could not get the hang of how the backhoe or bulldozer worked.

T.J. knew he was different because he knew the controls on most of the big machines like the back of his hand. His father had told him that using the backhoe was like riding a bike: once you learn how, you'll never lose your touch.

*backhoe バックホー；長いアームの先にバケットが付いた掘削機

## Questions about the story

1. Why was T.J.'s first job was on a construction site?
2. Where did he learn to use a backhoe?
3. What does his father do for a living?
4. What did the younger workers always start out doing?
5. What did the older workers usually think about the younger workers?
6. What made T.J. think he was different from the others?
7. What did his father say about learning how to work the backhoe?

## Questions for discussion

1. What are your hobbies?
2. What type of job would be right up your alley?
3. Have you ever thought about trying to turn your hobby into a job?
4. Have you ever been all thumbs at something?
5. What skills are similar to learning to ride a bike?
6. What would be a career that you think you would not be cut out for?
7. Describe a place you know like the back of your hand.

### バックホーへの道

幸せな人生を送る方法の一つは、趣味を仕事にすることだとT.J.は聞いていた。物心ついた頃からおもちゃのトラックやバックホーで遊んでいたし、大きな機械の操作は得意だった。父親はバックホーを持っていたので、何時間も掛けてその操作の仕方を見せてくれた。

T.J.の趣味にぴったりだったので、父の建設現場が彼の初めての仕事場だったことに親はまったく驚かなかった。最初は補助として、どこでも必要とされれば普通のシャベルを使って手伝った。こうして若手の新人が見習いをするのだった。ほとんどの新人は最初から機械の操作をするには未熟過ぎると先輩の作業員は思っていた。小さかったころ、T.J.は大きな機械の操作に必要な技能を持っていない若手の作業員の話を聞いていた。工事現場から帰ってきた父は、不器用でバックホーやブルドーザーの操作に慣れない若い作業員の話をしてくれたのだった。

T.J.は大きな機械の操縦装置に熟知していたので、自分は人とは違うと分かっていた。バックホーを使うのは自転車に乗るのと一緒で、一度やれば出来なくなることはないと、父が教えてくれたのだった。

# Memory & Loss

25 記憶と喪失

**forgive and forget**
to forgive and no longer dwell on or blame someone for a past mistake.
過去のことはさらりと水に流して忘れる；憎みを抱かず、許して忘れる。

兄弟同士はお互いに憎しみを抱いてはいけないので、アレックスは子供達のジェームズとライアンに forgive and forget しなさいと言った。
Alex commanded his children, James and Ryan, to forgive and forget, as brothers should not hold a grudge.

**fade away**
to become faint as time goes on.
消えて行く；消え去る。

若いカップルの辛い別れの記憶は時と共に fade away する。
Memories of the young couple's bitter breakup will fade away as time passes.

**draw a blank**
to be unable to remember information or think of something momentarily.
情報が得られない；答えられない；思い出せない；頭が真っ白になる。

ジェフは draw a blank していた…ショッピングセンターで昔の同級生に会った時、彼の名前を思い出せなかった。
Jeff was drawing a blank… he couldn't remember his former classmate's name when they bumped into each other at the mall.

### slip one's mind
to have forgotten; to not remember momentarily.
すっかり忘れる；度忘れする；思いつかない。

3時に医者と会う約束をしていたことを slip my mind した。
My appointment to meet with the doctor at three o'clock had slipped my mind.

### pop into one's head
to suddenly remember.
急に思い出す；思い浮かぶ；ふと思い出す。

質問を読み直していると、テストの答えが pop into Amy's head し始めた。
The test answers began to pop into Amy's head as she read over the questions.

### keep in mind
to constantly remember or think of.
～を心に留めておく；～を覚えておく。
*Synonym* bear in mind.

友達と自転車で出掛ける時は、すぐに暗くなることを keep in mind しなさいと母はサリーに言った。
Sally's mother told her to keep in mind that it would get dark soon when she went for a bike ride with her friends.

### look back (on)
to recall the past; to ponder memories.
～を思い返す；～を振り返る；～を思い出す。

幼かった頃のことを look back on すると、家族の経済的な問題にも拘らず私は結構、幸せだったと思う。
As I look back on my early childhood, I think that I was quite happy despite some of the financial difficulties that our family had.

### learn something by heart
to memorize.
暗記する。

小学校で、子供達は learn the national anthem by heart して、クラスメイトの前で歌わなければならなかった。
In primary school, the children had to learn the national anthem by heart and sing it with their classmates.

### hold on to
to keep; to not forget.
〜を離さない；〜にしがみついて；〜を手放さない；に固執する。

初めての彼女との楽しい思い出を私は未だに **hold on to** している。

I still hold on to the fond memories I have of my first girlfriend.

*This idiom most commonly precedes 'feelings,' 'thoughts' or 'memories.'
この慣用句は'feelings,' 'thoughts'または'memories'の前に用いることが一番多いです。

### cry over spilled milk
to get upset about something bad that has happened, but cannot be changed as it is in the past.
済んでしまったことを悔やむ；無駄なことで泣く。

あなたが欲しかった書類は昨日ゴミと一緒に出されたから **cry over spilled milk** しないで。

The papers you wanted went out in yesterday's garbage, so don't cry over spilled milk.

### be on the tip of one's tongue
to be ready to say something, but unable to remember it at the moment; to be just about to remember something that needs to be said.
〜が喉まで出かかって；口に出す前に思い留まって；思い出しそうとして思い出せない。

先月、私達が行ったあのレストランの名前は **be on the tip of my tongue** だが、思い出せない。

The name of the restaurant we went to last month is on the tip of my tongue, but I can't remember it.

# Fill in the blanks with the appropriate idioms.

**01** Old age is slowly catching up with Grandpa; his memory is beginning to _____ _____.
老化が段々と祖父に襲い掛かって来ている。記憶が段々と消え始めている。

**02** Someone needs to tell Jake that he is all grown up and that _____ _____ _____ his high school glory days as football quarterback is a waste of time.
もう大人だから、高校時代にアメフトのクォーターバックだった時の黄金時代にいつまでもしがみ付いていても無駄だと誰かがジェークに言わないといけない。

**03** When you travel to a foreign country, you should always _____ _____ _____ that you are not at home and that local customs may be very different from what you are used to.
外国へ行く時は、自分の国にはいないので、現地の習慣は自分のそれとは違うかもしれないと言うことを必ず覚えておく必要がある。

**04** Although it was on _____ _____ _____ his _____, Phil couldn't remember the name of his first girlfriend.
喉まで出かかっていたが、フィルは初めての彼女の名前を思い出すことが出来なかった。

**05** Danny _____ _____ total _____ as soon as he received his year-end final test paper.
学年末試験の問題用紙を渡された途端、ダニーの頭は真っ白になった。

**06** The lyrics for the song 'Let It Be' suddenly _____ _____ my _____ last night as I went to bed.
昨日ベッドに入ろうとしていた時に'Let It Be'の歌詞が急に頭に思い浮かんだ。

**07** As Susan _____ _____ _____ her choice to leave her boyfriend, she was filled with regret.
彼氏と別れると決めたことを思い出した瞬間、スーザンの胸は後悔で一杯になった。

**08** John really loves the rock group called U2. He _____ most of their songs _____ _____.
U2と言うロックグループをジョンは本当に大好きだ。彼らのほとんどの歌を暗記している。

**09** For months I was angry with my brother for borrowing my car without permission and causing it to break down, but now I realize that I need to _____ _____ _____.

私に許可を得ずに車を借りて故障させたことで、私は数ヶ月間弟に怒りを感じていたが、今、私はそのことを忘れて許してあげる必要があると気付いた。

**10** Jennifer's father said that there was nothing she could do to fix her broken doll and that she should stop _____ over _____ _____.

壊れた人形は直せないから無駄なことで泣くのを止めなさいとジェニファーの父は言った。

**11** Even though he had practiced for the interview for several days, when the interviewer asked Don to describe himself, everything he had rehearsed ___ his _____.

何日間も面接に備えて練習をしたにも拘らず、面接官に自分がどんな人なのか説明しなさいと言われた時、ドンは練習していたことを全て度忘れしてしまった。

**Answers** 1. fade away  2. holding on to  3. keep in mind  4. (on) the tip of (his) tongue  5. drew a (total) blank  6. popped into (my) head  7. looked back on  8. learned (most of their songs) by heart  9. forgive and forget  10. crying (over) spilled milk  11. slipped (his) mind

# Read the following story and refer to the questions below.

### - Reunions and Recollections

As Julian walked into the old gymnasium, he could not believe how small the space actually was. He looked back on his high school years as he passed the banners hanging on the wall. He couldn't get over that it had been twenty years since his team won the regional basketball championship and he graduated high school. Now he was here for his twenty-year reunion.

Over the last five years, some of the high school memories he had been holding on to had begun to fade away, one by one. As he walked through the doors, so many of the old memories popped into his head. A wave of emotion came over him. The good memories all came back, but so did the bad ones.

He remembered the many dances he attended and how he and his friends had learned all of their favorite bands' songs by heart. Julian remembered the time his girlfriend broke up with him at the spring dance and how upset he was. He realized later that he was crying over spilled milk that night. It had taken him a while, but he eventually learned to forgive and forget about that heart-breaking time.

Julian knew he was going to be terrible at recalling the names of his former classmates. He wanted to keep in mind the yearbooks\* that he had looked at back at his hotel room. As he approached the table to sign-in, he drew a total blank. One of his old girlfriends was sitting at the table and he could not remember her name. It was on the tip of his tongue, so he turned around to try and remember. Just then, she called Julian's name and introduced herself.

\*yearbook 卒業アルバム；年鑑

## Questions about the story

1. What could Julian not get over?
2. What event made him look back on his high school years?
3. What happened to some of his high school memories during the last five years?
4. What was one good memory that Julian had about his friends?
5. Describe one bad memory that came back to him and how he dealt with it.
6. What had he done to help him recall names at the reunion? Was he able to keep them in mind?
7. What happened to him as he approached the sign-in table?

## Questions for discussion

1. What are your best and worst memories of high school?
2. How could you describe what happened to some of your other high school memories?
3. What techniques do you use to recall names of people you have not seen in a long time?
4. How would you describe being upset over something trivial?
5. How would you describe something that you can't quite recall?
6. Did you ever draw a total blank at an interview or on a test? How did you deal with it?
7. Describe a time when something was on the tip of your tongue but you couldn't remember it.

### 同窓会と思い出

昔の体育館へ入って行った時、その狭さにジュリアンは驚いて信じられなかった。壁に掛かっているすだれを見て、高校時代のことを振り返った。自分が属していたチームがバスケットボールの地方大会に優勝して、高校を卒業した時からもうすでに20年も経っているということを受け入れられなかった。今は20年後の同窓会に参加するために来ていたのだ。ここ５年の間、ずっと離さずに抱いていた高校時代の記憶が一つづつ消え始めていたのだ。ドアをくぐって入って行った時にいくつもの思い出がふと思い浮かんだ。感情の高波が彼を襲った。良い思い出と一緒に辛い思い出も思い出したのだ。彼が行った数々のダンスパーティーのことを思い出しながら、友達と大好きなバンドの歌詞を全て暗記していたことも思い出した。春のダンスパーティーで彼女に振られた時の辛さも思い出した。あの晩は無駄なことで泣いていたのだと後で気付いたのだ。少し時間は掛かったが、そのうち、そのつらい思いを忘れて、彼女を許すことが出来た。

昔の同級生の名前を思い出すのはきっと難しいだろうとジュリアンは思っていた。ホテルの部屋で見ていた卒業アルバムを頭の中にとどめておきたいと思った。受付をするためにテーブルへ近づいた瞬間、頭が真っ白になった。昔の彼女がそこに座っていて、彼女の名前を思い出すことが出来なかった。喉まで出かかっていたので、思い出そうと彼は反対を向いた。ちょうどその時、彼女はジュリアンの名前を読んで、自己紹介をしてくれた。

# Chapters 21 - 25

Review Chapters 21-25 and fill in the crossword below.

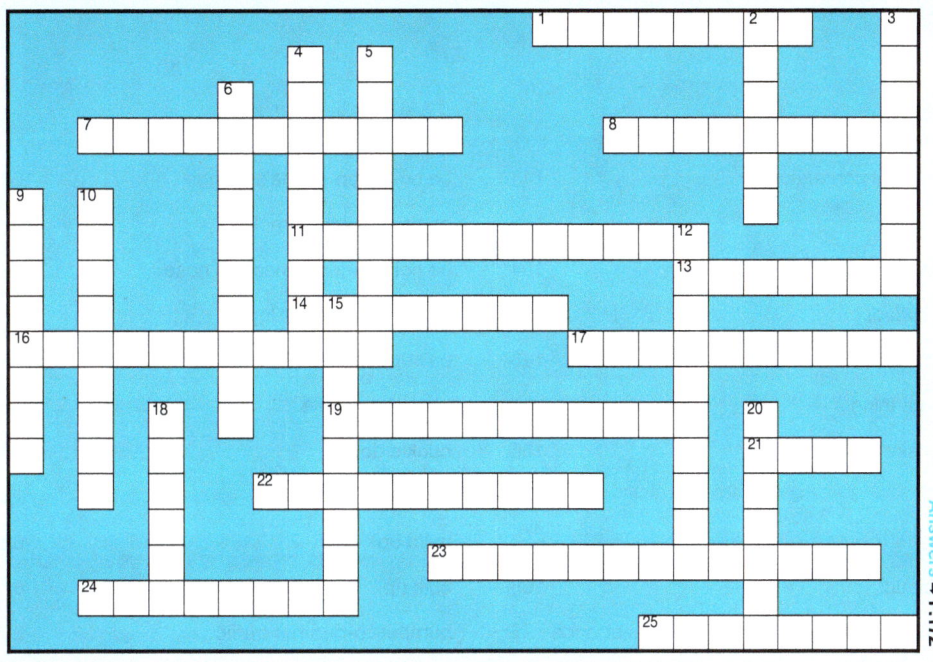

## Across

01. When I _____ _____ on my childhood, I think of all the things I wish I had known.
07. Obama _____ _____ _____ when he failed to respond to the situation in Bosnia.
08. The name of that band is on the _____ of my _____.
11. Sure, but if we _____ _____, we can get it done faster.
13. A prison escape? Well that's right _____ my _____.
14. Beth, you can _____ and _____ all you want, but you're not going to a rave party at 16.
16. The reporter _____ the _____ on the mayor for taking bribes.
17. I don't care what Jimmy called you. It takes _____ _____ _____.
19. I was willing to _____ _____ _____ on a new broker finding me good investments.
21. Mary _____ _____ knack for leading lambs. They'd follow her anywhere.
22. The Vikings won, but it was _____ _____ _____ for a bit. It was a close game.
23. I _____ over _____ for you and you won't even help me? You ingrate!
24. We _____ _____ with the neighbors about their loud music.
25. Jim had an _____ to _____ with his father for losing his inheritance in a poker game.

## Down

02. Cory loved his country, but he just wasn't _____ _____ for the Army.
03. The beauty of a young maid will soon _____ _____.
04. Ned is a _____ _____. I'm sure he'd help you.
05. Jeff laid it all _____ _____ _____ in the poker game and lost everything.
06. Please _____ _____ _____ that your papers will soon be due.
09. To get ahead in the movie business, you have to _____ _____ with big money people.
10. I had a _____ _____ coming to work. I almost got hit on my bike.
12. Anytime you drink and drive, you _____ _____ _____ of killing someone.
15. I would never be a good surgeon. I'm _____ _____.
18. I cannot recall the date of the meeting; it slipped _____ _____.
20. I tried golf, but I just can't seem to get _____ _____ of it.

Memory & Loss 165

# Index

インデックス

## A

| | |
|---|---|
| a bone of contention | 143 |
| acid test | 109 |
| a greenhorn | 154 |
| all-aut(adj.) | 85 |
| a real sport | 148 |
| a sure thing | 97 |
| at stake | 136 |

## B

| | |
|---|---|
| back up | 108 |
| balls in the air; juggling many things at once | 96 |
| bark up the wrong tree | 91 |
| be after | 79 |
| be all thumbs | 153 |
| bear in mind | 159 |
| be cut out for | 153 |
| be dying for | 118 |
| be iffy | 95 |
| be in on | 103 |
| be in shape | 60 |
| be in the way | 125 |
| be itching for; have a hankering for | 118 |
| be long gone | 49 |
| bend over backwards | 148 |
| be none of someone's beeswax | 125 |
| be none of someone's business | 125 |
| be off | 48 |
| be on a diet | 62 |
| be on the tip of one's tongue | 160 |
| be on the wrong track | 89 |
| be right under someone's nose | 24 |
| be right up one's alley | 153 |
| be supposed to | 120 |
| blow the whistle | 143 |
| buckle down | 113 |
| buckle up | 29 |
| build up | 62 |
| bulk up | 62 |
| bumper-to-bumper traffic | 28 |
| bundle up | 17 |
| burn the candle at both ends | 85 |
| burn the midnight oil | 84 |
| busybody | 125 |
| butt in | 125 |
| by foot | 24 |

## C

| | |
|---|---|
| call dibs on | 119 |
| call the shots | 130 |
| carpool; rideshare | 29 |
| catch one's breath | 62 |
| catch someone's eye | 67 |
| cause a stir | 142 |
| chances are (that) | 95 |
| check out | 23 |

| | | | |
|---|---|---|---|
| chip in | 72 | don't go with | 17 |
| climb on the bandwagon; hop on the bandwagon | 108 | do something over | 89 |
| | | double-park(ing) | 29 |
| close call | 135 | drag one's feet | 85 |
| close shave; be too close for comfort | 135 | drag one's heels; drag one's ass. (slang) | 85 |
| come across | 79 | draw a blank | 158 |
| come by | 79 | draw up | 42 |
| come on strong | 114 | dress up | 17 |
| come out in favor of | 108 | drive like a maniac | 36 |
| come together | 147 | drive like crazy | 36 |
| come up with | 79 | drop someone/something off | 28 |
| cook up | 42 | | |
| cool down | 61 | **E** | |
| could do with | 118 | early bird | 55 |
| could go for | 118 | | |
| count someone in | 103 | **F** | |
| count someone out | 103 | fade away | 158 |
| cross one's mind | 67 | faux pas | 90 |
| cry over spilt milk | 160 | feel like | 118 |
| cut it out; quit it | 125 | fifty-fifty | 95 |
| cut someone/something off | 36 | fight a losing battle | 96 |
| | | fill up | 36 |
| **D** | | find out | 79 |
| dash off | 48 | fold up | 17 |
| dawn on | 67 | follow something through | 114 |
| digest (information) | 68 | forgive and forget | 158 |
| do a favor | 148 | | |
| do a good turn | 148 | | |

## G

| | |
|---|---|
| gas-guzzler | 36 |
| gas-hog | 36 |
| get around | 35 |
| get around to | 84 |
| get changed | 17 |
| get down to it | 113 |
| get dressed | 16 |
| get going | 48 |
| get in shape | 60 |
| get in(to) | 35 |
| get lost | 125 |
| get off (of) | 35 |
| get off someone's back | 124 |
| get off someone's case | 124 |
| get one's second wind | 114 |
| get one's wires crossed | 91 |
| get on someone's back | 124 |
| get on someone's case | 124 |
| get on(to) | 35 |
| get out and about | 54 |
| get out of | 35 |
| get the feel for | 154 |
| get the hang of | 154 |
| give it one's best shot | 114 |
| give someone a bum steer | 73 |
| give (someone) a lift | 29 |
| give someone a push in the right direction | 73 |
| give (someone) a ride | 29 |
| give (someone) a speaking to | 73 |
| go all out | 85 |
| go away; take a hike; beat it; scram; hit the road | 125 |
| go for a cruise | 34 |
| go for a drive | 34 |
| goof up | 89 |
| go on a diet | 62 |
| go out of one's way | 30, 149 |
| go over | 78 |
| go overboard | 113 |
| go with | 17 |
| grow out of | 18 |

## H

| | |
|---|---|
| had better | 119 |
| halfhearted | 85 |
| hand-me-down | 17 |
| harp on | 142 |
| have a ball | 53 |
| have a blast | 53 |
| have a green thumb | 154 |
| have a hand in | 103 |
| have an ax to grind | 141 |
| have a (real) knack for | 154 |
| have (got) dibs on | 119 |
| have got to | 119 |

| | | | |
|---|---|---|---|
| have it out (with) | 141 | **K** | |
| have on | 16 | keep in mind | 159 |
| have one's pick | 130 | keep (it) up | 85 |
| have to | 120 | knock it off | 125 |
| have to fly | 37 | know something/someone like the back of one's | |
| have words (with) | 141 | hand | 154 |
| head for | 23 | knuckle down | 113 |
| head off | 48 | | |
| head out | 48 | **L** | |
| help someone out | 72 | lay off | 61 |
| hit the gym | 61 | learn something by heart | 159 |
| hit the road | 49 | leave something open | 130 |
| hold on to | 159 | leave something (up) to | 130 |
| hop in | 35 | left out | 102 |
| hop off (of) | 35 | lend someone a hand | 72 |
| hop on(to) | 35 | life of the party | 54 |
| | | live it up | 53 |
| **I** | | live life in the fast lane | 53 |
| in the line of fire; on the front line | 136 | long for | 118 |
| in the works | 43 | long shot | 97 |
| irons in the fire | 96 | look back (on) | 159 |
| it takes two to tango | 148 | look into | 78 |
| | | look on | 103 |
| **J** | | look out (for) | 67 |
| join in | 103 | look up | 78 |
| jump on the bandwagon | 108 | lose one's touch | 154 |

## M

| | |
|---|---|
| make a big deal of | 142 |
| make a mess of | 90 |
| make a mountain out of a molehill | 142 |
| make good time | 36 |
| make room for | 24 |
| make up one's mind | 129 |
| make waves | 143 |
| map out | 43 |
| mess up | 90 |
| mind one's own beeswax; butt out | 124 |
| mind one's own business | 124 |
| miss out (on) | 95 |
| miss the boat | 97 |
| miss the bus | 97 |
| mix up | 90 |
| move over | 23 |

## N

| | |
|---|---|
| night on the town | 54 |
| night owl | 55 |
| nitpick | 142 |
| nosy-parker, meddler | 125 |
| not have a leg to stand on | 109 |
| not lift a finger | 85 |
| not think straight | 91 |

## O

| | |
|---|---|
| odds are (that) | 96 |
| off the cuff | 42 |
| on foot | 24 |
| on one's way | 29 |
| on the line | 136 |
| on the spur of the moment | 43 |
| out of breath | 62 |
| out of shape | 60 |
| out of the woods | 136 |

## P

| | |
|---|---|
| paint the town red | 54 |
| paper trail | 109 |
| party animal | 54 |
| pass by | 24 |
| pass up | 96 |
| pay attention (to) | 68 |
| pick and choose | 129 |
| pick up | 28 |
| pipe dream | 96 |
| pitch in | 72 |
| play ball (with) | 147 |
| play it by ear | 43 |
| play it safe | 135 |
| pop into one's head | 159 |
| pros and cons | 129 |
| pull for | 109 |

| | | | |
|---|---|---|---|
| pull together | 148 | settle on | 130 |
| put all one's eggs in one basket | 96 | share a ride | 29 |
| put on | 16 | shoot for the moon | 114 |
| put one's foot in one's mouth | 90 | show up | 102 |
| put on weight | 61 | sink in | 68 |
| put your heads together | 148 | sit out | 102 |
| | | sit up straight | 24 |

**R**

| | | | |
|---|---|---|---|
| | | skate on thin ice | 136 |
| rally around | 72 | slip of the tongue | 90 |
| rant and rave | 141 | slip one's mind | 158 |
| reach for the stars; shoot for the stars | 114 | sneak off | 49 |
| read up on | 80 | sound someone out | 73 |
| ride on someone's coattails | 109 | speak to | 73 |
| ride shotgun | 35 | split hairs | 142 |
| ring a bell | 67 | stand a chance | 96 |
| risk one's neck | 135 | stand behind | 109 |
| road rage | 29 | stand out | 68 |
| rock the boat | 143 | stand up for | 108 |
| root for | 109 | steer someone straight | 73 |
| rule of thumb | 130 | step up | 113 |
| rule out | 42 | stick one's neck out | 135 |
| run across | 79 | stick one's nose into | 125 |
| run the risk of | 135 | stir up a hornet's nest | 142 |
| rush hour | 28 | | |

**S**

**T**

| | | | |
|---|---|---|---|
| | | tailgate | 36 |
| screw up | 89 | take a chance | 136 |
| set of wheels | 37 | take a spin | 34 |

| | |
|---|---|
| take in | 68 |
| take it or leave it | 130 |
| take note (of) | 68 |
| take off | 16, 37, 48 |
| take one's pick | 130 |
| take part in | 103 |
| take the bull by the horns | 84 |
| take turns | 147 |
| take under one's wing | 73 |
| take up | 24 |
| team up (with) | 102, 148 |
| the chips are down | 136 |
| think up | 79 |
| throw a party | 54 |
| throw caution to the wind | 136 |
| to be short of breath; lose one's breath. | 62 |
| to each his own | 119 |
| touch and go | 135 |
| traffic jam | 28 |
| tread in dangerous waters | 136 |
| tread on thin ice | 136 |
| trim down | 61 |
| try on | 16 |
| turn back | 23 |
| turn to | 72 |
| turn up | 79 |

## U

| | |
|---|---|
| up in the air | 43 |

## W

| | |
|---|---|
| warm up | 60 |
| wear out | 18 |
| wet behind the ears | 154 |
| wheels | 37 |
| wing it | 43 |
| words of wisdom | 73 |
| work off | 62 |
| workout | 61 |
| work with | 147 |
| would rather | 119 |

# Crossword Answers

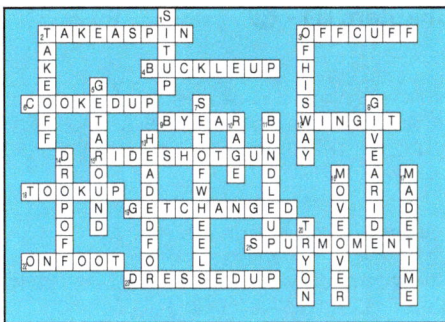

### Chapters 1 - 5

**Across**

2. TAKEASPIN  3. OFFCUFF  4. BUCKLEUP
6. COOKEDUP  9. BYEAR  12. WINGIT
15. RIDESHOTGUN  18. TOOKUP
19. GETCHANGED  21. SPURMOMENT  22. ONFOOT
23. DRESSEDUP

**Down**

1. SITUP  2. TAKEOFF  3. OFHISWAY  5. GETAROUND
7. SETOFWHEELS  8. GIVEARIDE  10. RAGE
11. BUNDLEUP  13. HEADEDFOR  14. DROPOFF
16. MOVEOVER  17. MADETIME  20. TRYON

### Chapters 6 - 10

**Across**

1. PAINTRED  5. HITTHEROAD  6. SNUCKOFF
8. LOOKOUT  10. PUTON  11. WORKOFF
13. ONADIET  15. SOUNDOUT  18. HEADOUT
19. TOOKNOTE  20. DAWNEDON  21. GETGOING
22. STEERSTRAIGHT

**Down**

2. TOOKOFF  3. LIVEUP  4. CATCH
7. THROWAPARTY  9. TURNTO  12. FASTLANE
13. OUTANDABOUT
14. PITCHESIN  16. GETINSHAPE  17. RINGSABELL

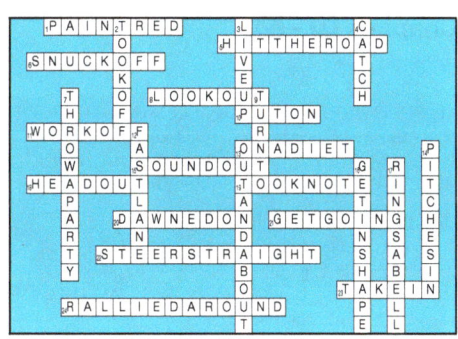

### Chapters 11 - 15

**Across**

3. LIFTAFINGER  6. AROUNDTO  7. LOOKINTO
10. THINKSTRAIGHT  11. MIXUP  12. CHANCESARE
14. COMEACROSS  15. LEFTOUT  19. SURETHINGS
20. DRAGGINGFEET  21. PASSUP  22. SITOUT
23. JOININ  24. TURNUP  25. ISAFTER

**Down**

1. COUNTIN  2. MIDNIGHTOIL  4. FOOTINHISMOUTH
5. CAMEUPWITH  8. DOOVER  9. STANDCHANCE
13. KEEPUP  16. GOOFEDUP  17. MISSBOAT
18. AHANDIN

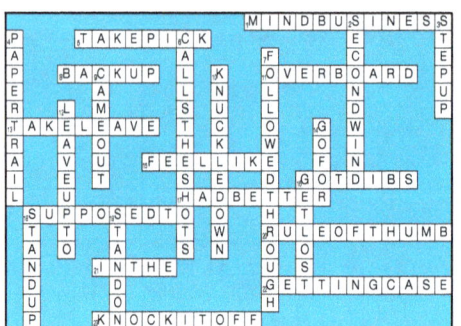

## Chapters 16 - 20

### Across
1. MINDBUSINESS  5. TAKEPICK  8. BACKUP
11. OVERBOARD  13. TAKELEAVE  15. FEELLIKE
16. GOTDiBS  17. HADBETTER  18. SUPPOSEDTO
20. RULEOFTHUMB  21. INTHE  22. GETTINGCASE
23. KNOCKITOFF

### Down
2. SECONDWIND  3. STEPUP  4. PAPERTRAIL
6. CALLSTHESHOTS  7. FOLLOWEDTHROUGH
9. CAMEOUT  10. KNUCKLEDOWN  12. LEAVEUPTO  14. GOFOR  16. GETLOST  18. STANDUP  19. STANDON

## Chapters 21 - 25

### Across
1. LOOKBACK  7. CAUSEDASTIR  8. TIPTONGUE
11. PULLTOGETHER  13. UPALLEY  14. RANTRAVE
16. BLEWWHISTLE  17. TWOTOTANGO
19. TAKEACHANCE  21. HASA  22. TOUCHANDGO
23. BENTBACKWARDS  24. HADWORDS

### Down
2. CUTOUT  3. FADEAWAY  4. REALSPORT
5. ONTHELINE  6. KEEPINMIND  9. PLAYBALL
10. CLOSECALL  12. RUNTHERISK  15. ALLTHUMBS
18. MYMIND  20. THEHANG

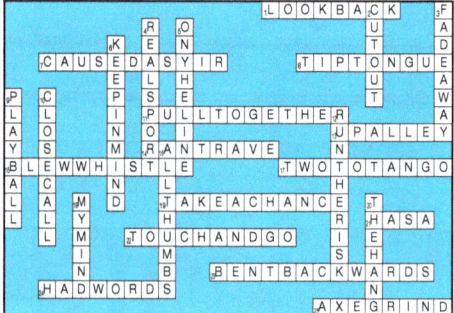

# Dedication & Copyright

「This book is dedicated to the love of language,
to the warp of words & twisted meaning
and to the art of deciphering them.」

Copyright © 2017 by Peter Liptak
The authors assert the moral right to be identified as the authors of the work. All rights reserved. No part of this publication may be reproduced in any form, or by any means, electronic or mechanical, including photocopying, recording or any information storage and retrieval system, without the written permission from the publisher.

ISBN 978-1-936342-52-5
eBook 978-1-936342-53-2
Idiom Attack Vol. 3: Taking Action (Japanese Edition)
イディオム・アタック 3 行動を起こそう
Exile Press LLC
2355 Fairview Avenue North, #191
Roseville, MN 55113

Library of Congress Control Number: 2017907043
Cataloging-in-Publication Data
Liptak, Peter N.
Idiom Attack Vol. 4: Getting Emotional / by Peter N. Liptak, Matt Dauma & Jay Dauma.
1st ed.
p.174 cm. 24.4
Includes table of contents and index
ISBN 978-1-936342-52-5 (alk. paper)
1. English language – Idioms  2. Japanese language  3. Americanisms
4. English language – Terms and phrases – dictionaries – Japanese.
I. Title
LC Classification: PE1689 .L57 2017
Language Code: engjap

Exile Press LLC
www.ExilePress.com

www.ingramcontent.com/pod-product-compliance
Lightning Source LLC
Chambersburg PA
CBHW050500110426
42742CB00018B/3325